# Government and Business

# GOVERNMENT PROSPECTS
## AND FOR
# BUSINESS PARTNERSHIP

Edited by Kirsten Dodge

Lyndon B. Johnson School of Public Affairs
Lyndon Baines Johnson Library
1980

# Contents

# Contents

# Foreword

The relationship between government and business—especially between the federal government and the nation's large corporations—has traditionally been an adversary association. The tension between the two entities is perhaps inevitable, as government's regulatory and taxing functions naturally run contrary to business's primary objective of increased profits. But with the unending pressure of inflation and the increasing tendency of the American public to distrust "big business" and "big government" alike, the need for improved communication and cooperation between the public and private sectors has become critical.

In March 1979 representatives of business, government, and academia were brought together in Austin, Texas to discuss the rationale and potential for partnership. The two-day symposium was sponsored jointly by the Lyndon Baines Johnson Library, the Lyndon B. Johnson School of Public Affairs, the Graduate School of Business of The University of Texas at Austin, and the Institute for Constructive Capitalism, a research organization of the Graduate School of Business. This book contains the proceedings of that symposium, which was considered by all in attendance to be a positive contribution to the business-government relationship.

The volume is designed so that those lacking the time to read the text in its entirety can benefit from its major points. A summary precedes each section, and within the text significant statements are extracted and placed in bold type at the bottom of the pages on which they appear. Thus, by concentrating on summaries, the extracts, and the descriptive subheadings provided in the speeches and discussions, a reader can follow the flow of the proceedings and glean whatever is of individual interest or use.

The symposium was planned by a coordinating

committee that included Harry Middleton, Director of the Lyndon Baines Johnson Library; Elspeth Rostow, Dean of the Lyndon B. Johnson School of Public Affairs; George Kozmetsky, Dean of the UT Austin Graduate School of Business and the College of Business Administration; Liz Carpenter, representing the Lyndon Baines Johnson Foundation; Walt W. Rostow, Professor of Economics and History, The University of Texas at Austin; Timothy W. Ruefli, Professor of Management and Associate Director for Research, Institute for Constructive Capitalism, UT Austin Graduate School of Business; and Kathryn Green, also of the Institute for Constructive Capitalism.

The arduous task of creating a readable text from the symposium transcripts was placed in the capable hands of Kirsten Dodge, a faculty member of the UT Austin College of Business Administration and a freelance editor. It is Ms. Dodge who appears throughout the book as the "narrator," providing summaries, biographies, and overviews as they are needed.

Publication of the volume was funded in part by the Lyndon Baines Johnson Foundation, through the Lyndon Baines Johnson Library. Production was handled by the Lyndon B. Johnson School of Public Affairs Office of Publications.

It is hoped that these proceedings will recapture for a large group of readers the spirit of optimism and cooperation that pervaded the symposium, and that it will provide the impetus for further examination of this important issue.

# I Keynote

**Felix Rohatyn**
*Partner,*
Lazard Frères & Company

*Felix Rohatyn began his career with Lazard Frères & Company, investment bankers, in 1948. He served as chairman of the New York Stock Exchange's surveillance committee in 1970, and was credited with keeping the brokerage business alive through a time of crisis. He has been a director for International Telephone and Telegraph Corporation, Pfizer Company, Owens Illinois, Inc., and Howmet Corporation. He is a trustee of Middlebury College, Vermont, his alma mater, and serves on the Board of Directors of the New York City Heart Association. He turned from these duties to the financial problems of New York City. As the Chairman of the Municipal Assistance Corporation he labored successfully to solve the problem of New York City's debt. He is now special economic adviser to the Governor of New York.*

## Solving Intractable Problems Through Partnership

I was brought into public life by a great son of your state, Bob Strauss. Like anybody who has been in touch with Bob Strauss, I have my own Bob Strauss story. I had had breakfast with Bob in late May, '75, when the city was obviously going to go bankrupt.

1

Strauss said to me, "What do you think will happen if New York goes bankrupt?"

I said, "Bob, I think it will be a catastrophe."

About a half an hour later, I had a call from Governor Carey, who said, "I'm glad to hear you volunteered to help us in trying to keep the city out of bankruptcy."

So I called Strauss, and I said, "Strauss, what is this?"

And he said, "Well, you just take a couple of weeks off and do this; it will be interesting and challenging."

So I said, "Okay."

Two weeks, three weeks. About a year and a half later, I called Strauss: the end was absolutely nowhere in sight.

And I said, "Strauss, how could you do this to me?"

"Well, Rohatyn," he said, "saving New York City is like making love to a gorilla.

"You don't stop when *you're* tired," he said, "you stop when the *gorilla's* tired."

That was three and a half years ago.

## New York City Headed For Catastrophe

In May 1975, New York City was headed for bankruptcy. Government alone was clearly unable to stop the process. At neither the city, the state, nor the federal level could one find the determination, know-how, and means to prevent a catastrophe.

This was equally true, however, of the business community, especially my own community, the financial community. Having financed the city to excess, the financial community was unable to solve the problem.

At stake was the solvency not only of New York City, but of the State of New York. An aggregate of over thirty billion in securities could default—representing, then, approximately twenty percent of the capital of the United States banking system.

---

**"The implications of such a mammoth bankruptcy went ... beyond our own economy and could severely threaten the dollar—and with it the international monetary system."**

The implications of such a mammoth bankruptcy went, in my judgement, beyond our own economy and could severely threaten the dollar, and with it the international monetary system. Federal officials, who had no solutions, pretended there were no major problems. Local officials pretended the problem would go away if the banks would only provide credit. The banks, having lent too much, said, "Enough is enough."

## Government and Private Sectors Join Forces

Governor Carey, at that point, turned to the business community, and we, in turn, joined hands with labor. New structures came into being: structures that represented the joining of forces of government and the private sector.

The Municipal Assistance Corporation (MAC) was created to finance the city. The Emergency Financial Control Board (EFCB) was created to bring the city's budget into balance. In the case of MAC, a state agency with a board of directors consisting solely of private citizens appointed by the governor was given control over one and a quarter billion of annual tax revenues against which it could issue bonds. In the case of the Control Board, a board consisting of the governor, the mayor of the city, the state comptroller, and three private citizens was given the power of approval over the city's budget.

Since then, MAC has provided the city with over ten billion of financing on its own—and spearheaded the city's efforts to obtain federal guarantees for another 1.65 billion. The Control Board has provided the pressure to bring the city's budgetary deficit down from an annual level of approximately two and a half billion a year to approximately one half billion now. And if things keep on going reasonably well, to a balanced budget within the next three years.

MAC and the Control Board were instrumental in such unpopular but necessary decisions as the institution of tuition at City University; a thirty percent increase in transit fares; a wage freeze and wage deferral program with the city's unions; a twenty percent reduction in the work force; approximately $100 million a year shift of pension costs from the city over to the labor force; and, long before Proposition 13 became fashionable, a cap followed by downward pressure on property-tax rates.

We haven't solved all of our problems in New York City. Far from it. But in a relatively finite period of time a runaway, seemingly intractable problem of vast dimensions was brought under control. More importantly, the direction and philosophy of a large unit of government was fundamentally and permanently changed as a result of the involvement—some would say intrusion—of the private sector in government. In my judgment, this is a principle that is applicable to a vast array of national problems, for reasons not too dissimilar to the New York experience.

It is this conviction that led me to accept with great pleasure the opportunity to address this very important symposium. The United States today is in many ways similar to New York City in 1975: the loss of private-sector jobs; the year-after-year deficits; lowered productivity; higher and higher taxes; reliance on short-term debt to avoid facing tough issues; hidden liabilities in the form of unfunded pensions and social security.

All of these sound terribly familiar to those of us who wrestled with New York City. What is the difference, after all, between the Republic National Bank in Dallas refusing to buy New York City notes and the reluctance of the Swiss Bank Corporation to hold United States dollars?

Both are making judgments not only about the soundness of the credit, but about the underlying strength of the economic unit, and equally important, about the effectiveness of its political leadership.

The involvement of private citizens in the affairs of New York City, in partnership with government officials, clearly avoided a potential disaster that neither the private sector nor government, alone, was capable of solving. One has only

---

**"The direction and philosophy of a large unit of government was fundamentally and permanently changed as a result of the involvement—some would say intrusion—of the private sector in government."**

to look at the problems of Cleveland to see what can happen when such partnerships fail to jell. Cleveland went into default, and may yet sink into bankruptcy and chaos, because the mayor and the business community are at loggerheads.

Luckily for us a default of Cleveland, involving some fifteen to twenty million, is irrelevant from a financial point of view. But for the people who live there it can turn out to be catastrophic. It is also a political disgrace.

There was no need for Cleveland to go into default. The means were there to prevent it; the talent was there to find alternatives. It happened because there was no will, no dialogue, no structure that encompassed, under one roof, local government and the private sector.

## Under One Roof: Business, Government, and Labor

In referring to the private sector, I include labor as well as business. The actions taken to save New York City required legislative actions, both in Albany and Washington, as well as massive financing. Without the political support of the municipal unions, neither MAC nor the Control Board could have come into being. The opposition of local politicians would have been too great. Over the last four years union pension systems acquired several billions of our bonds. But at least as great a contribution was their political support at the local and national levels.

In addition, what may be the most important structure of all came into being almost by chance. After a particularly virulent clash between the city, the unions, and the banks, communications broke down. Walter Wriston, Chairman of Citibank, Jack Bigel, representing the municipal unions, and I began talks that resulted in an informal group with the rather quaint acronym of MUFL, which stands for Municipal Unions-Financial Leaders. (You would think with all this combined power, one could come up with something a little more poetic.)

At regular intervals this group, consisting of the heads of the main clearinghouse banks, the leaders of the unions, and the chairman of MAC, takes joint positions in areas where they can agree. Welfare reform and tax reductions for business were two examples. If you don't think that municipal labor supporting high-bracket tax reduction in Albany is revolutionary, then you'd better think again.

Equally important is the fact that we discussed everything of importance to the city and the state, including areas where the unions and the banks can't possibly agree institutionally. City and state officials, occasionally including the mayor and the governor, regularly attend and participate in these sessions. The importance of this exercise is in the area of mutual understanding. Tensions between these critical financial and political power centers at times of crisis have been considerably reduced. Personal relationships of respect and understanding have been created, where previously suspicion and mistrust turned every problem into confrontation. The lowered decibels in the public arena permitted political accommodation without loss of face, an impossibility a few years ago.

Four years ago, when Governor Carey drafted me in our fight against bankruptcy, I had literally never met a city or state official, a local union leader, a newspaper editor. I was in a complete state of virginity, municipally speaking. Today that virginity lies tattered at my feet. But like all erstwhile virgins, I have learned a lot: about government, local and national, about labor, about politics, and about the media.

This experience, which I wouldn't have missed for anything in the world, nonetheless causes me deep concern about the ability of our governmental institutions, alone, to cope with our problems; skepticism about the ability of our political system to survive if those problems aren't faced; and a conviction that solutions, if any, can only come about in cooperation between government and the private sector, and in structures that combine the best of both.

Western democracy, is without any question, the noblest as well as the most delicious form of government

---

**"Personal relationships of respect and understanding have been created where previously suspicion and mistrust turned every problem into confrontation."**

ever invented. It may, however, be a luxury that requires an abundance of resources which may be on the point of running out. It is worth considering, at a time when expectations have been rising everywhere in the Western World, whether democracy could survive an extended period of austerity and reduced standard of living, except in wartime. And yet, with many of our governmental institutions paralyzed or inept, with overregulation and bureaucracy stifling the basic entrepreneurial drive of business, austerity is where we are headed if we are lucky. Much worse if we are not.

## Major Danger Areas For Western Democracy

What are some of the major danger areas at this point, and why would a business-government partnership help? First and foremost is probably energy. In one of the most pathetic examples of political impotence and national lack of will, the United States, following the clear warning of the oil embargo of 1973, is more dependent on imported energy than ever. We cannot afford major supply interruptions without an industrial crisis; we cannot maintain the status quo indefinitely without our banking system becoming hostage to OPEC. An all-out domestic energy production program, in addition to stringent conservation measures, is an absolute necessity. It requires both price deregulation and new institutions to speed the process along.

It has seemed to me for some time that a national energy development bank, or alternatively, a series of regional development banks, should be created to deal with projects too large or risky for the private sector alone. They should have powers of expediting the process of siting, permits, state by state differentials, et cetera.

---

**"Western democracy is, without any question, the noblest as well as the most delicious form of government ever invented. It may, however, be a luxury that requires an abundance of resources which may be on the point of running out."**

In the Northeast we have been working on just such a project for three years. We are about to reintroduce legislation in the United States Senate. Encono, the Energy Corporation of the Northeast, will have equity capital of a billion dollars, owned by the seven northeastern states. The corporation will have the right to issue $15 billion in bonds to be guaranteed by the United States Government. It will be managed by a board of directors of private citizens appointed by the governors and run by professionals hired by the board. It will operate in partnership with private companies and is not permitted to own or finance more than fifty percent of any project. It will have the power to expedite projects and, through its relationship with the governors and the states, will have considerable political leverage. It should be the catalyst for projects too large or risky to be undertaken alone, and will turn over its investments as projects become commercially viable.

Our cost of energy in the Northeast is two and a half times the average of the rest of the country, since we are so dependent on imported crude. Lowering that cost by switching to domestic production will help the fight against inflation, help the fight to protect the dollar, and create jobs and revenues. In addition, if this project gets congressional approval, we should attempt to interest some of the OPEC countries in purchasing Encono's federally guaranteed bonds, thus recycling petro-dollars on a long-term basis with a project that would lengthen the life of their own reserves.

If Encono sees the light of day, it will have considerable Texas parentage, since Walt Rostow from this school has been of enormous help to us as mentor, adviser, and friend. And we shan't forget it.

Both the concept of Encono, bringing it along to this stage, and running it when launched, are products of business-government cooperation. Having seven states agree on anything is miraculous. In this case seven states agreed on a concept by having each governor appoint one person from the private sector and one person from his own staff as his representative. This group of fourteen developed the concept over a period of several months, then reported back to the governors, who blessed it and staffed it. A bill was introduced last year, sponsored by all the region's senators, Senator Jackson, and other important senators. I think that Encono, like MAC, is a classic example of business-government cooperation.

I had the privilege of acting as Governor Carey's representative. Bill Miller, who is now chairman of the Fed, was the governor of Rhode Island's representative. This was a concept that came about in partnership, away from political tensions. The corporation, if it comes into being, will run like a business. But it will be publicly accountable because of its gubernatorial appointments and treasury oversight.

The concept of regional development banks, combining private management with public funding and accountability, is applicable in areas other than energy. Whether it's Western water problems, Southern rural industrialization problems, Northeast and Midwest energy problems—a particular region's problems can be attacked more vigorously and more effectively in this fashion.

## Tasks Facing This Country Today

The tasks this country faces are monumental. But tackling them vigorously would provide jobs and the revenues that will be needed if the social infrastructure is to be maintained. In addition to energy, I think we need a railroad system that is viable. We need to bring private employment to the inner-city ghetto, which is probably becoming a more dangerous bomb than anything the Russians can throw at us. We need clean air and rivers. None of these programs, which offer great challenges as well as great opportunities, can even be conceived of without not only business-government partnership, but business-government-labor partnership. It simply can't be done.

A different area in which a business-government partnership can pay big dividends is rather far removed from actual day-to-day operations. It consists in helping to create a public climate which permits political leaders to make unpopular decisions without committing hara-kiri. Equally

9

important is permitting action—as opposed to endless delays, equivalent to ultimate vetoes—of project after project through the actions of militant minorities.

Again I look back on our experience in New York City. As much as anything else, the influence that the private members of MAC and the Control Board exerted was on the political process itself. This was due to the public support we gained as a result of a supportive press.

**A Supportive Press**

Early on we made a fundamental decision to be totally candid with the press. It was a decision that entailed risk, since we were continuously teetering on the brink of bankruptcy. The press, however, once it understood what we were trying to do and why, treated us with fairness, supported us, and created the climate in which political leaders could do difficult and painful things. Tuition at City University, transit fare increases, service reduction, the entire budget balancing process, consists of one unpopular decision after another. Not only could politicians do difficult things; it also turned out to be good politics. Governor Carey's popularity never stood so high as after that long summer of 1975 when, together with us, he led the fight against bankruptcy.

Business-government cooperation already exists on a large scale at the local government level. New York City may have been an extreme case, brought on by an emergency, when private citizens actually participated to a considerable extent in the governmental process. In many other cases the cooperation is less formalized, but nonetheless effective. Businessmen, after all, provide jobs, capital spending, et cetera. The political sector is increasingly in need of increased revenues without increased taxes. Business activity is clearly the best answer.

For the cooperation to be as effective as possible, and for it to be raised to the national level as opposed to the local level, businesspeople will have to make efforts of their own and undertake certain risks. By and large, business leaders have been ready and willing to serve government as opposed to working with government. As Cabinet members and commission chairmen, Presidential advisers and ambassadors, they have served the country well. They are usually timid, however, about getting involved in politics, and, through the media, in taking public positions on a variety of issues.

It is an understandable position. Politics is probably the cruelest form of activity known to man, short of war and cannibalism. Not as cruel, but equally risky, is the involvement with the media. There is always the possibility of embarrassment, of making people angry and attracting fire from various quarters. There is possibly the greater danger of getting hooked on being a public figure, of believing that your own inane statement, because you read it in *The New York Times*, is all of a sudden imbued with wisdom. However, if business leaders are to play the role they can and should play, in a world increasingly in need of sanity, they will have to come out of the closet and deal with politics and the press.

Labor leaders, far better than those in business, understood long ago that involvement in public affairs and a direct relationship with the media were powerful instruments for getting political attention. Business leaders who wish to make an impact have to do the same. Their views may have the wisdom of Solomon, but only if they have the editorial support of the *Times* and the *News* will they become public policy.

### Political Impotence and Bureaucratic Ineptness

Increasingly today, the problems of government are twofold: political impotence and bureaucratic ineptness. Business-government cooperation can help in both areas.

Political impotence is the result, in great measure, of the paralysis caused by splinter groups exercising veto power at every level of government. The concept of democracy has

---

"Politics is probably the cruelest form of activity known to man, short of war and cannibalism. Not as cruel, but equally as risky, is the involvement with the media."

been distorted to permit the will of various minorities, through manipulation of the legislative as well as the judiciary process, to turn what should be review processes into vetoes by delay.

If that were not enough, excessive regulation, coupled with a normal amount of bureaucratic ineptness, has added layer upon layer of cost to an economy already struggling to contain inflation and remain internationally competitive.

A change in political climate is needed to cope with political paralysis. Involved business people, in partnership with labor, can have an impact at the grass-roots level and provide political leaders with a platform for action.

Increasingly, as we face the possibility of a serious economic downturn, as well as runaway inflation, the creation of jobs and the maintenance of purchasing power will be the issues of the day.

Most business people understand that there is more to business than just profits; that there is a moral imperative for affirmative action, social responsibility, and environmental protection. But it must take place within the framework of a viable, ongoing economic and social unit, and with the recognition that, for the business people and their companies, tomorrow always comes.

The business leader, if he has credibility and is willing to take the risks, can be of enormous help to the political leader in creating a climate in which it is possible to break through log-jams and to act. In New York State, a council of business and labor leaders, which I have the privilege of chairing, has just been appointed by the governor to try to overcome the straitjacket in which many of our more significant economic projects find themselves. Whether it be new power plants,

---

"Increasingly today, the problems of government are twofold: political impotence and bureaucratic ineptness. Business-government cooperation can help in both areas. Political impotence is the result, in great measure, of the paralysis caused by splinter groups exercising veto power at every level of government."

industrial parts, or a convention center, they need an enormous push. We intend to do just that.

With respect to bureaucratic ineptness, business can contribute by participating in the creation and management of new, mixed structures which are bound to come into being. Whether in local structures like MAC, regional structures like Encono, or national structures of a similar nature, business and government can circumvent bureaucracy as well as take certain well-defined tasks out of the political tug-of-war that government agencies are subject to.

Jean Monnet changed the face of postwar Europe with his vision of such structures. The European Coal and Steel Authority and EURATOM were the kind of structures in which government and business joined hands for a specific task. Their impact, however went far beyond the task itself, and resulted in new perceptions and understandings which brought forth the European currency union.

The suggestion that government and business join hands in new structures invariably brings the cry of socialism, New Dealism, et cetera.

I must confess to you, in the interest of full disclosure, that I grew up as a New Deal liberal. When I came to this country as a refugee, during World War II, Franklin Roosevelt was my hero, the New Deal an unparalleled intellectual achievement. I believed in government's ability to manage, to right wrongs and make things work. I was also, obviously, totally ignorant of government and its functioning.

Today, I am neither liberal nor conservative, but profoundly skeptical. The fact that I find government, at any level, neither inspiring nor efficient does not, however, lead

---

**"With respect to bureaucratic ineptness, business can contribute by participating in the creation and management of new, mixed structures which are bound to come into being....Business and government can circumvent bureaucracy as well as take certain well-defined tasks out of the political tug-of-war that government agencies are subject to."**

me to conclude that one can do without it. It leads me to the conclusion that it has to be encouraged to inspire and helped to be efficient.

### Primitive Economic Slogans

We live with primitive economic slogans today, most of which cannot stand the test of reason. They are the result of television newscasting which turns complex problems into two minutes with Walter Cronkite, and public officials selling themselves to voters with thirty-second commercials on the same news program. Some of these slogans have become conventional wisdom.

The concept of a "service economy," for instance, strikes me as a simple cop-out. It merely says, "these are the current tides and there is nothing we can do about it." These are indeed the current tides, but there is much we should do about it. I believe that no industrially developed society can function for long unless the main part of its economic activity comes from the production of goods. The "service economy" concept is justified by the "free trade" religion. But is it really in this country's interest to run tens of billions of dollars of balance of trade deficits with Japan, destroy the value of our dollar (which, incidentally, works to their advantage by reducing their costs of fuel), and decimate some of our manufacturing industries? I think that proposition is arguable.

As a result of these slogans, today's political and economic philosophies seem to oscillate between two equally unsatisfactory schools of thought: the neo-conservative thesis of "government is inept, therefore, the less government does, the better it is," and the liberal thesis of "we can afford anything as long as we print money."

The former is intellectual bankruptcy; slicing the salami ever thinner will not solve the problems of a country of a

---

**"If we really want a constitutional convention to stop inflation, let us provide that no elected official can run for reelection when the consumer price index rises more than six percent."**

quarter of a billion people with a rapidly growing permanent underclass.

The latter will lead to actual bankruptcy, in the form of runaway inflation—which we are approaching by leaps and bounds as it is.

We must be able to come up with answers other than a constitutional convention for a balanced budget, a thirty percent across-the-board tax cut, or national health insurance. If we really want a constitutional convention to stop inflation, let us provide that no elected official can run for reelection when the Consumer Price Index rises more than six percent. That would get my vote.

In the meantime, however, we have to be more active, innovative, and aggressive in dealing with energy, productivity, exports, inflation. We have to link the legitimacy of government with what is left of entrepreneurship if we are to maintain our political system. I believe, with every fiber of my being, that what this country faces is not a bigger or smaller recession or more or less inflation, or a stronger or weaker dollar. Those are all effects; they are not causes. What we face is the possible loss of our most precious asset: Western democracy, surely the most magnificent form of organized life ever invented.

What we face today is war at home. War with inflation, with unemployment, with lack of education, with racial discrimination. A war which we are, furthermore, not winning. If we lose, our system of government may not survive. Whether we wind up with left-wing or right-wing authoritarianism is irrelevant. Poison is as lethal served from the left as from the right.

We in New York City found ourselves at war and created the equivalent of coalition government to manage an austerity program. It is a coalition of government, business, and labor. And it works. A similar coalition must be created

---

**"What we face is the possible loss of our most precious asset: Western democracy, surely the most magnificent form of organized life ever invented."**

at the national level if we are to show the rest of the world that our system really works where it should: at home.

There are risks, of course, in any course of action. But the risk of inaction today is clearly greater. Action carries with it the risk of failure, which is hateful. Failing without trying, however, is despicable. The concept of partnership carries risks both for government and for business, but the risks must be taken. The destiny of countries was never shaped by fatalists.

# Summary:
# Keynote

Felix Rohatyn covered all the important issues: the bankruptcy of New York City and its implications, the problems of the railroads, energy, the regulatory agencies, the tasks and dangers facing Western democracy.

He demonstrated, through his account of the timely rescue of New York City, that when business thinking is brought to bear on a catastrophic situation like that of New York City, with enough authority to make its analysis felt, then the specific steps needed to bring things back into balance can be marked out.

It may be remarked, however, that collaborative action of any kind demands an object. In the case of New York City it was to avert a catastrophe. But the objective of business is not to avert a catastrophe; it is to serve the interests of a market and compete with others in doing so and still make a profit. Is the case of New York City, then, unique?

Is anything in the experience of New York City broadly applicable to the problems besetting the nation? Is collaboration among disparate institutions—business, government, labor, academia, the press—possible or even desirable in other than times of crisis? How are problems defined, objectives set, and steps to solutions begun?

It is questions like these the speakers and panelists of the conference seek to answer.

# II Rationale for a Business-Government Partnership

Introduction: **Robert O. Anderson,**
Chief Executive Officer,
Atlantic Richfield Company

Moderator: **George Kozmetsky,**
Dean, College of Business Administration,
The University of Texas at Austin

Panelists: **Leonard Silk,**
Economic Columnist,
*The New York Times*

**W. Donham Crawford,**
Chief Executive Officer,
Gulf States Utility Company

**Douglas M. Costle,**
Director,
Environmental Protection Agency

**William I. Spencer,**
President,
Citibank of New York

# Summary:
# Rationale for
# Partnership

The rationale for partnership among four major sectors of American society—business, government, labor, and academia—seems, to the first group of panelists, to be no less than the survival of a vigorous, free, economically sound America.

Impeding or even opposing the realization of such a partnership is public distrust of big business and big government. And yet such a partnership may be needed to solve severe national problems akin to those faced and dramatically solved by the business-government-labor alliance in the case of New York City.

Skepticism toward government and business has resulted in what is called a "breakdown in civil dialogue" among Americans. Public distrust of both spheres is matched by hostility and distrust between business and government themselves, caused primarily by the "regulatory morass." Cost-benefit studies and careful estimates of the social costs of regulatory actions prior to legislation are suggested as possible means for controlling the growing web of regulations and promoting more cordial relations between business and government.

American business, it is agreed, has shown increasing social responsibility in the last twenty years. But some of American business's lack of credibility might stem from the traditional reluctance of American business leaders to articulate their concerns publicly or to involve themselves in the political process.

A theme recurs throughout the first discussion: to forge new problem-solving relationships among different sectors of American society, Americans must identify a common goal. Conflict of interest and factionalism need to be controlled, not through legislation, but through ethics and an attitude of concern and involvement on the part of the people. The media especially must be kept free of special interests if Americans are to be provided with the facts needed to think about and solve complex national problems.

If different sectors borrow each other's tools to attack deeply interconnected problems, might they not end up with some of the others' problems? This panel makes a beginning in exploring a partnership among traditionally opposing sectors of American society.

# II Rationale for a Business-Government Partnership

**Robert O. Anderson**
*Chief Executive Officer,*
Atlantic-Richfield Company

*Robert Anderson has been Chairman of the Board and Chief Executive Officer of Atlantic-Richfield Company since May 1965. He began his career in oil in 1939, working for American Mineral Spirits Company. During the next two decades he bought and expanded refineries, including Wilshire Oil Company of California, all later sold to Gulf Oil Corporation. Mr. Anderson currently owns Lincoln County Livestock Company and is Chairman of Diamond-A Cattle Company, both of New Mexico. He served as Chairman of the Board of the Federal Reserve Bank of Dallas from 1961 to 1964. He is an active benefactor of many institutes, and is Chairman of the Aspen Institute of Humanistic Studies in Colorado.*

## Responsibility in a Free Society

The foundation of our society in the eighteenth century was based on a simple revolutionary concept: free people working together could create a world which they could direct. And it could be created and directed in such a way that tomorrow would offer a better day than today.

Up until that time people tended to look backwards in their lives, because tomorrow was the unknown. Tomorrow

23

carried the virtual certainty that it would have problems one would like to avoid.

This idea of free people working together in a democratic society was so revolutionary that it was almost inconceivable. To make sure that it worked, we were given a brand new continent, one that had hardly been touched. The people who had lived in North America were an agrarian, food-gathering society, and they left it to us as they had found it.

In two hundred years we have done quite a job of plundering it. We have done a great job of enjoying it. Its wealth may be the very thing that has spoiled us. Because we had enough in this society we could argue, we could fight, we could have intellectual disagreement. And it was a very productive argument. But we have probably reached the point where we can no longer afford this. At least we can no longer afford undisciplined disagreement.

In a democratic society one functioned under what was called at that time the "Social Contract." According to the Social Contract, the minority must consent to be governed by the majority. If you can become the majority, the minority in turn must consent to your government. There was a clear cut, implied obligation on the part of the minority to support the majority if the objectives of a democratic society were to be achieved.

### A Factionalized Society

We, today, have become a highly factionalized nation. In the Federalist Papers there is a great section devoted to the dangers of factionalizing a democratic government such as our own. When we're wealthy we have plenty to go around; we did have plenty, with our great farming capacity.

---

"Because we had enough in this society, we could argue, we could fight, we could have intellectual disagreement. And it was a very productive argument. But we have probably reached the point where we can no longer afford . . . undisciplined disagreement."

Robert O. Anderson    *Introduction*
Atlantic-Richfield Co.

One time we had nearly exclusive management of the fine tools in the world: technology. Most of the products of any sophistication that moved abroad were produced in this country. We were under no urgency. We really had it made. But today we're in a world that is highly competitive. The American laborer, the working person, may work with tools that are inferior to those used in many places in the world.

Now one might ask, how did this happen? How did we move from a society in which our American workers enjoyed the best tools, the best working conditions, to one that can no longer say it is number one?

### Members of the Partnership

To talk about a new partnership between business and government would be meaningless, unless labor is considered as an equal, in every sense of the word, in any dialogue we undertake. While I have sat on the other side of the table from labor people on many occasions, nevertheless I see the labor movement in this country as one of the great successes of this century.

If one looks around the world at labor movements in other countries, one begins to realize that we have been most fortunate in the development of unions in the United States.

With the triumvirate—business, government, and labor—plus the support of academia, we have the ability to move this society ahead. We can compete. We can face issues like the energy crisis. But we can't do anything as long as we retreat to our own positions, as long as we insist that somehow or other each segment should get more than the total.

### Constructive Dialogue

In the last thirty years we have seen the government sector grow at a prodigious rate. The government, in the pursuit of its own interest and its desires for new programs, particularly of a social nature, has drained a great deal of capital in the form of what could have been tools for the American worker.

25

We cannot continue to take more out of our society annually than we put in. We have done that now for far too many years.

I know of no issue that this country faces more urgent than establishing a serious, constructive dialogue among business, labor, and the public sector. The energy crisis may decide whether we are capable of acting. In five years we have literally gone backwards. We have not come to grips with the energy problem. Less than half of the people in the country are aware that there really is a crisis that could destroy the entire world we have created.

**Willingness to Take Risks**

One of our problems is the lack of willingness to take risks. No one wants to take risks, which are considered not only objectionable, but quite possibly expungeable.

We can't live without risks. We have to come with a way to evaluate them and decide which to take. Some of them are objectionable. But we have to do it. Coal, nuclear power—we must have energy if we're going to have jobs. I suspects jobs may be the bottom line for any society. Vertical mobility in employment, employment opportunities, horizontal mobility, freedom of choice of occupation: these are the things that truly make an open and productive nation.

We have had these benefits of an open and productive nation and we should do everything we can to maintain them.

The private sector offers the bulk of employment opportunities, and it offers the bulk of mobility. Unless we can keep jobs, interesting jobs, and a way of life that will support the majority of our American people, we won't have much. As Felix Rohatyn has said, whether you go toward the

---

"We have the ability to move this society ahead. We can compete. We can face issues like the energy crisis. But we can't do anything as long as we retreat to our own positions, as long as we insist that somehow or other each segment should get more than the total."

left or the right in an authoritarian government, it really doesn't matter. If democracy goes, all the values we believe in and cherish go with it.

There is a very interesting comment from the *Decline and Fall of the Roman Empire* relating to the Athenians. I can't quote it exactly—but it said when the Athenians cared less for responsibility and more for the material successes of their life, when they turned from responsibility, in the end they lost not only their freedom, they lost their way of iife.

We must as a nation put in as much as we take out. We have to put it together.

**George Kozmetsky**
*Dean,*
College of Business
Administration and
Graduate School of
Business,
The University of Texas
at Austin

*Dr. George Kozmetsky, in addition to being dean, is Director of the Institute for Constructive Capitalism at UT Austin. He serves the University of Texas System as Executive Associate for Economic Affairs. Before he came to Texas he cofounded and served as Executive Vice President of Teledyne, Inc., a California-based electronics firm. He has taught at the University of Washington, the Harvard Graduate School of Business, and the Carnegie Institute. His specialties include systems analysis, organizational theory, quantitative methods, information technology, and the study of capitalism.*

## Identifying Possible Partners

To provide a setting for the discussion to follow, let's concentrate on the word "partnership." A partner is one who has a share in or a part of something together with another. Both government and business have a share of a nation's resources. As each sector applies and distributes its resources, the way the other sector can fruitfully invest or administer its own resources changes. The sectors are partners in controlling the nation's wealth for the common good. The different sectors of society include not only government, business, and labor, but academia, but church, and all the nonprofit institutions of our society. Our institutions are under scrutiny today. We in this nation are at a crossroads: we are forming institutions to fit the needs of humans rather than fitting the humans to the needs of today's institutions.

George Kozmetsky
UT Austin

## Defining Partnership

Uncoerced human cooperation is essential if we're to review our nation's investment in all resources. Human cooperation increases productivity, provides for full employment, stabilizes prices, provides necessary means for foreign trade, increases the quality of life, and provides for public welfare and security. Cooperation can't be uncoerced until priorities are agreed to. Agreement on priorities depends on at least one overarching concern capable of generating interaction, not merely reaction.

Max Ways took me to task just a few months ago when I used the word "partnership" in front of him. By "partnership," I mean there should be an improvement in communication, talking to each other as well as hearing each other. Especially listening to each other. I do *not* mean by "partnership" a narrowing of differences by coercion between individual corporations or between various government agencies or between business and government. Both business and government should broaden their mutual areas of consensus; that is a positive partnership.

Basically, business firms and government agencies are competitive. Each has its own stated purposes, established individually in the case of business, and by statute as in the case of government.

Max Ways said: "Business, government, and academia all have separate social functions rooted in society's separate needs."

"I don't think," Max said, "they can be amalgamated without compromising both the freedom and the vigor of a society. Instead let these institutions keep their distance from one another and improve their communication across the distance. I know, of course, that in the real world there is no practical danger that the leaders of American institutions will coalesce in one big partnership."

---

"Cooperation can't be uncoerced until priorities are agreed to. Agreement on priorities depends on at least one overarching concern capable of generating interaction, not merely reaction."

Max Ways' remarks helped clarify my thinking. In the real environment we have an opportunity to act on our concern for our national well-being. We can accept that business, labor, government, academia, and others have concommittant ownership of and responsibility for our national resources. We can seal this new partnership by agreeing to sustain communication among the sectors, to share information voluntarily, and together to determine national policies and required priorities. The American people have always benefited most when business and government relations were good, yet each played its respective role.

**Communication and Resource Allocation**

Felix Rohatyn says, and I agree, that without full communication and cooperation, the technological resources of the business community and the mineral resources of the government cannot be applied simultaneously to meet the nation's energy needs.

As government policy affects business, communication increases on two levels: concrete information exchange and priority matching. President Carter's national energy plan is a valuable example because it represents a limited set of goals over which individuals or sectors may agree or disagree, and in doing so establish communication. The National Energy Plan has occasioned extensive investigation of the precise extent of our mineral resources and discussions about the importance of restoring our balance of trade and the limits of our national security.

If we as a nation of many parts are to achieve our national and international goals, restore our once healthy balance of trade, reduce unemployment, curb inflation, and provide for the general welfare, we must mobilize all resources—whether technological, natural, or human.

*Leonard Silk begins the following discussion by identifying some of the problems facing the country, including the value of the dollar and the role of the press. He also sums up the need of controlling our present bitter conflicts of interest, not with private or public programs but through a shift in attitude and a concentration on ethics.*

*Donham Crawford continues by clarifying the issues under scrutiny, sticking to the business he knows and using graphic illustrations to get across his points. He emphasizes even more clearly than does Felix Rohatyn the need for precise costing of all social and political aims.*

*Douglas Costle speaks on the issue of factionalization in this country and on the need to recreate public trust. William Spencer also speaks on the credibility problem, before the discussion becomes more freewheeling following the moderator's question: Has American business begun to change its political stance?*

**Leonard Silk**
*Editorial Board,*
*The New York Times*

*Prior to joining* The New York Times *as economic columnist in 1970, Dr. Silk was a Senior Fellow at Brookings Institute. He has been Chairman of the Editorial Board, as well as a writer, for* Business Week. *He also served as a member of the President's Commission on Budget Concepts. In addition to his work as a thinker, a journalist, and a commissioner, Dr. Silk has taught economics at such schools as Columbia University, Duke University, and New York University. Among his most recent published books are* Capitalism, The Moving Target *(1973);* Contemporary Economics *(1975); and* Economics in Plain English *(1978).*

## Ethics and Public Concern

We have a whole host of economic and political problems that are interlocking. The economic problem would be solvable if we would work together better. Or at least it could be for the life of all of us and probably for the lives of our children and grandchildren.

The strictly economic part of our interlocking problems includes the problem of inflation. Inflation is the most critical problem at the moment, as has already been mentioned by both Felix Rohatyn and Bob Anderson. Unemployment must not be forgotten, as Felix Rohatyn stressed.

Whether we call it unemployment or welfare or the underclass of the country, we cannot forget that there may be an explosion yet to come from that segment of society. We must never neglect it or forget it. If we *do* forget it, it will be to our terrible peril.

## The Value of Our Currency

Internationally, we have a whole host of issues business and government are involved in together. So we need to improve the relationship between business and government.

Economic problems all acquire a tag name: The Dollar. Certainly in its own specific terms the dollar is a very serious problem. Everything bears on it: the Iranian Revolution; the radicals not only within that country but in the surrounding countries; our trade relations with Western Europe and with Japan; the way we conduct our affairs at home, including inflation and productivity.

Everything comes to focus in one area: on the value of our currency. The value of our currency is a little bit like the American flag. It may not make very good sense, and economists who are devotees of floating exchange rates may not like things symbolically or emotionally interpreted, but I think it's true that the dollar is a quasi flag. When it sinks lower and lower, people assume that something is seriously wrong with America, and that something must be done or this country is going to the dogs.

George Kozmetsky asked us earlier to think about the current issues pertinent to government-business partnership. This is the kind of question you could go on and on about. But I do want to say a word about the political aspects of these problems, which go in every direction.

Internationally our might as a nation is very much involved. The inability of the country to command respect abroad may have a great deal to do with some of the

---

"The value of our currency is a little bit like the American flag.... When it sinks lower and lower, people assume that something is seriously wrong with America, and that something must be done or this country is going to the dogs."

problems we are currently facing in the economic and financial areas.

Domestically, we again have to pull together as a country. It's hard to figure out how to do that within our democratic system. It's not only that we have party against party. From the beginning, Washington and Jefferson and Madison, and so on, were willing to countenance different parties. I think that is the strength of the country.

But there are other kinds of divisions in the country that can be more lacerating. Conflicts between business and labor, between consumers and environmentalists, between blacks and whites, between Hispanic Americans and other Americans.

### Controlled Conflict of Interest

We have problems in the role of the press. This arm's-length relationship among sectors that George Kozmetsky was referring to, quoting Max Ways, is a very hard thing to sort out. To what extent are we to separate from one another and play separate roles, and to what extent are we to work together? This conference has a very important theme.

The name of the game is conflict of interest. That's the reason we of the press try terribly hard not to acquire additional responsibilities. Lately our executive editor has been telling the staff that he won't have them serving on presidential commissions; he won't have them testifying before Congress; he doesn't want them involved in any aspect of the news. That may be too pure a position, but maybe it's right for us. I don't know whether it's right for everybody else.

I think we've got to have conflict of interest, but it has to be controlled. Not by government per se, although government may sometimes get into the picture. Conflict of interest has to be controlled by ethics, by our moral sense of

---

**"Conflict of interest has to be controlled by ethics, by our moral sense of right and wrong. That is the only way a free society can handle the potential conflict of interest question."**

right and wrong. That is the only way a free society can handle the potential conflict of interest question, whether it is bankers serving on a municipal control board, or labor leaders doing the same or serving in government to help on energy policy.

We must rely on a sense of ethics, of public concern. A college course could be conducted on what we mean by ethics; I'm not going to try to resolve that here. But I submit to you that ethics are part of our central issue here. What is the ethical issue? What is the moral issue? What is the public, civic, interest that permits us, with our separate interests, to join together for worthy purposes?

**W. Donham Crawford**
*Chief Executive Officer,*
Gulf States Utility Company

*Donham Crawford's career in the energy industry dates from his service with the U.S. Atomic Energy Commission, Savannah River Operations Office, and includes experience with such companies as Middle South Utilities, Consolidated Edison of New York, and the Edison Electric Institute. He has also served in an advisory capacity to several federal agencies. For three years he was a member of the nation's Air Quality Advisory Board, and for four years he was Chairman of the Electric Utilities Advisory Committee of the U.S. Federal Energy Administration. He is currently Chairman of the Board and Chief Executive Officer of the Gulf States Utility Company.*

### Need for Partnership

I want to tell a little story about the government-industry partnership, because I think it illustrates some of the problems we're addressing.

Government regulations continue to play a major role in our energy situation. But regulations have a history of creating rather than solving problems. Take a small emerging nation in Africa, whose traditional English regulations required driving on the left-hand side of the highway. You can imagine the chaos this situation created when drivers reached the border. After a great deal of parliamentary debate, it was decided to change from the left-hand side to the right-hand side.

W. Donham Crawford
Gulf States Utility Co.

But in order to compromise with the opponents of the change, Parliament mandated that for the first week the rule would only apply to trucks.

Now, if this reminds you of some of the compromises reached during last year's national energy legislation, the coincidence is intended.

The need in this country for a new business-government partnership, is, in my view, beyond question. The kind of business-government partnership I would like to see, and that I think is in question, is one in which the government would be a limited partner. Before you tag me as one who wants to turn the clock back, let me say that I not only recognize but want a role for government in business. In fact, in my industry, the electric utility industry, it's absolutely essential. But I maintain that government's role should be to contribute to the conduct of business rather than to inhibit it—as it does so frequently.

## Social Cost of Government Action

What I'd like to do is to sketch a few guidelines for this new industry-business partnership. One of the things that must be done, somehow, is to embue in the government a greater realization of the social costs of its actions. Ideally this should be done before legislation is enacted, before regulations are promulgated, or before programs are put into place. But that's not always possible.

We need some reliable methodology to test and to evaluate the cost of existing legislation as well as proposed legislation. We must somehow get into the habit of making cost-benefit studies. This is certainly not a new idea; it's been around for a long time. But government historically has been unwilling to use cost-benefit analysis.

I want to cite a recent example of what I mean by cost-benefit allocations. I want to make it clear that I'm not trying to hang this all on the Environmental Protection Agency. After all, they're implementing the laws that Congress adopts. What I'm going to talk about has to do with some amendments to the Clean Air Act of 1970, concerning the removal of small incremental amounts of pollutants from

37

exhaust gases. The proposed regulations would have required the installation of very expensive and, for the most part, technically immature devices that scrub the gases coming out of the stack.

The cost of the standards as they have existed is $19 per ton of particulate removed; the cost of the EPA proposal is fifteen times higher, or $282 per ton. Unfortunately, the impact of this proposal was to reduce the emissions by only one percent. What we have are proposed regulations, with a cost increase of fifteen times that of previous standards, to remove one percent of the pollutants.

In America today there is a growing web of confusing, frequently contradictory, and always time-consuming government regulations aimed at everything from job safety to nuclear-waste disposal. And nowhere has this tightening web had a more devastating effect that on the electric industry and its ability to provide our country with needed supplies of electric power. I confine myself to just a couple of examples.

The legislative and regulatory morass surrounding nuclear power is indeed mind boggling. On the one hand, we say, and the President says, that we must have nuclear power in order to meet our electric power requirements. And that's right.

But on the other hand we outdo ourselves in inhibiting its development and its use. The President last year proposed legislation to speed reactor licensing, but the proposal bogged down. The proposal finally lapsed at the end of the Congressional session because of objections from anti-nuclear, antienergy, antigrowth, and thus antijob zealots in the Administration. Many of these zealots were appointed to their positions by the President. Where nuclear power is concerned, our ability to use it is very much in question.

---

**"In America today there is a growing web of confusing, frequently contradictory, and always time-consuming government regulations aimed at everything from job safety to nuclear-waste disposal."**

W. Donham Crawford
Gulf States Utility Co.

I would say to you that if the nuclear option is effectively destroyed, its death will have been brought about by slow governmental strangulation, not by any lack of desire on the part of the electric utility industry to use nuclear power for the benefit of consumers—not the least benefit of which is the shelter nuclear power provides against rising oil prices.

## Responsibility on Intervenors

I contend that intervenors responsible for delaying demonstrably needed energy facilities should be held financially accountable for the added costs of the delays if their case is ultimately found to lack merit.

A good example of this concerns a company I was formerly with, Consolidated Edison Company of New York. About fifteen years ago the company made a proposal to install a pump-storage facility, needed for peak purposes in New York City, at a place called Cornwall on the Hudson River. The plant has been delayed repeatedly by a small group of well-heeled individuals, mostly property owners and environmentalists. It still has not been built. If it is ever built, there will be a tremendous additional cost which must be borne, not by the intervenors in the project, but by the ratepayers of Consolidated Edison Company.

Those intervenors should bear some part of the cost. Although my lawyer friends tell me that this may not be possible because it might deny due process of law, I remain unconvinced. To allow the intervenors for their own, rather narrow purposes to delay such a facility, in effect allows a small special-interest group to define the public interest de facto.

If, subsequently, the public interest turns out to be something other than what they said it was, then it seems to me that there should be some recourse for recovering the invariably large costs resulting from the delays. To put it in more prosaic terms: Why should an elderly customer of Consolidated Edison Company, on a fixed income, have to pay many more times the cost of electricity because a group of intervenors was able to hold up a needed power plant for fifteen years?

We also ought to be able to find some way to expedite the judicial appeal. Applications for important energy facilities languish for years in the courts. I'm not sure what the answer is. Perhaps it would be to provide a special new court with very limited appeal rights, and expedited treatment for appeals, to adjudicate the difficult and complex energy versus environmental disputes. The new government-industry partnership should consider that.

I'm not simply talking about delays and frustrations, but about a big price tag. Economist Murray Weidenbaum says it may approach $109 billion this fiscal year.

**Building Public Confidence**

Ever since the first partnership on earth, the partners have been at each other's throats on one matter or another. The business-government relationship is no exception. Nor, some would argue, should it be. A healthy, free society presupposes conflicting interests, with government playing the role of moderator. That was James Madison's view in the Federalist Papers in 1787. I agree with it, but I can't help but wonder if the nation wouldn't be better served if the partners, business and government, could somehow find a way to resolve their differences other than through shouting matches.

Business is certainly as much to blame here as government. We are every bit as strident and as political in our allegations about government bureaucrats and legislators as they are about our alleged avarice and self-interest.

Mind you, I'm not suggesting that government should mask their honest differences with a perennial posture of sweet reasonableness. Obviously, there are and will continue to be fundamental differences. Both sides of a given issue need to be fully aired.

---

**"Ever since the first partnership on earth, the partners have been at each other's throats on one matter or another. The business-government relationship is no exception. Nor, some would argue, should it be."**

W. Donham Crawford
Gulf States Utility Co.

A word about business responsibilities in this new era: I would hope that business would have a larger role in the public policy process, but that larger role is by no means guaranteed. Paradoxically, we must earn it by accepting what appears to be a limited responsibility—that of a team player rather than a star.

William Sneath, the chairman of Union Carbide, recently said: "Our goal is not to dominate the system but to strengthen it. That means helping to build public confidence that the system works for everyone. Only by doing that can we retain the right to take part."

This remark admirably describes in a few words the way for business to approach the new partnership. It is the key to establishing a successful business-government partnership.

**Douglas M. Costle**
*Administrator,*
Environmental Protection
Agency

*Douglas Costle began his federal service in 1964 as a trial attorney in the Civil Rights Division of the U.S. Department of Justice. Shortly thereafter he became a staff attorney for the Economic Development Administration of the U.S. Department of Commerce. By the beginning of 1970 his attention had settled on two areas: environmental protection and government organization. He served in several environmental agencies and was a member of President Carter's transition team on government organization before assuming his current task of Administrator of the Environmental Protection Agency.*

## Institutions Interconnected

I don't think there is anyone who would disagree that, whether we want it or not, we are in partnership.

Our society and our institutions are interconnected and interlocked in very complicated ways—a web of relationships that in fact represents a partnership. It may not be one we understand very well, and it certainly is one that needs to be infused with fresh vision and vigor.

More difficult, I think, is the question of what are the requisites for that infusion of fresh vigor and vision. What is it, in short, that's necessary if the public is to see partnership as credible?

## Facing a Breakdown in Civil Dialogue

There was a wonderful phrase that Bob Anderson used: undisciplined disagreement. Perhaps because of the era from which we are now emerging, the Watergate period, there has been in a sense a breakdown of civility, or civil dialogue. It's a far more complicated thing than I could hope to penetrate. It's the sort of thing that Leonard Silk was beginning to get at in his comments.

Bob Anderson also used the word "factionalized"; that's another key word. People are particularly distrustful of the large institutions in their lives. We live in a complex technological society. We generate and convey information at enormous speed and in enormous volume.

I'll bet there isn't anyone in this room who can remember what they saw in the evening news, or remember two out of three stories that they saw on the evening news not three nights ago. Or what was said about those news events. Perhaps we're approaching an information overload. So much information is confusing people. They don't know how to sort out the facts.

There is also a sense in this country that we lack institutions that can integrate our society and integrate these facts and this information. The large institutions that have done that for us in the past, be it business, government, or the church, simply have less credibility today, for a variety of reasons, than they did even twenty years ago.

Even the universities have failed. If there is an integrating institution in our country, you would think it would be the university. In the university you bring all of these marvelous disciplines together, and you try to connect thoughts and ideas and information.

But I remember a conversation with a Nobel physicist at Harvard many years ago. He said when he started in physics it was possible for him to keep abreast of what was going on on the frontier of his discipline. And even several other disciplines.

By the time he and I were speaking in about 1960, he said this: "I can barely now keep apace of the emerging developments in my narrow discipline alone, let alone other natural science disciplines. I cannot keep abreast of what's going on any longer in biochemistry or in any of a series of disciplines."

He added, "If you think that's a difficult thing to come to grips with, my ability to communicate with my colleagues in the social sciences is almost nonexistent."

So there has been even at the universities, an increasing balkanization of discipline and of information and of the pursuit of knowledge. The universities struggle with how to integrate into some sort of whole social fabric the very vigorous pursuits and increasingly narrow disciplines and subdisciplines.

Ironically, it's probably true that in a democracy, like it or not, the government—our elected leadership, the Congress and local governments, state governments, and the institutions that the Congress establishes to implement laws—serves as an integrator. The government attempts to take changing social values and the changing nature of the social contract, and, as a group of elected representatives, amend that contract on a continuous evolutionary basis. The government tries to implement those laws in the form of adjustments in the contract that will be acceptable to the people.

**Recreating Public Trust**

Given people's lack of faith in government, and lack of faith in business, and in our big institutions, how do we make partnership credible in their minds, and not simply an unholy alliance? How do we make this partnership credible—as they see it? This is the biggest difficulty in achieving what Felix Rohatyn and Bob Anderson were talking about.

I think we must start with the recognition that we do live in an era of changing values, and as a nation we are searching for a perspective. We are attempting in many ways to rediscover what our fundamental values are.

I think an absolute first requisite, if a partnership is to have credibility, is for the public to trust us. We must,

---

**"Given people's lack of faith in government, and lack of faith in business, and in our big institutions, how do we make partnership credible in their minds, and not simply an unholy alliance?"**

together and separately, recreate trust in people's minds in the institutions that govern their lives. That is very difficult to do because they are a skeptical lot today.

We live in an era of extraordinary skepticism. What I see as perhaps the most distressing fact of all is the withdrawal of people from the political process. I think before television we routinely used to get seventy percent of eligible voters to the polls. We're now well below fifty percent.

I fear more than anything that people will withdraw, and that it will become even more difficult to reestablish the trust we need to legitimize a partnership that in fact our nation does need. I think that the withdrawal, if it occurs, will leave us in confusion and disarray. And that troubles me deeply.

---

**"We must, together and separately, recreate trust in people's minds in the institutions that govern their lives."**

45

**William I. Spencer**
*President,*
Citibank of New York

*William Spencer is President of Citibank of New York and a board member of Citicorp, a federal corporation chartered by Congress. When Mr. Spencer assumed his responsibilities as President and Chief Administrative Officer of Citibank, he brought to bear years of work with specialized industries, particularly the petroleum industry. In addition to serving as a member of the National Advisory Committee on Banking Policies and Practices, he is a director of Sears Roebuck and Company, United Technologies, Asia Pacific Capital Corporation, Odyssey Institute Incorporated, and the Transportation Association of America.*

## Credibility Problem

This inability of any of us in business or government to be credible is probably—as Douglas Costle touched on—our greatest problem. The ability of splinter groups to deter, to change the direction of, or to stop vast programs winds up costing the very people involved a great deal. Someone mentioned the Con Edison situation. He didn't mention that at the same time Con Edison was unable to get approval to put an oil-burning plant in Brooklyn, it was publicly and privately castigated as the evil author of a blackout in the city.

We in business are dramatically at fault for the misunderstanding. Because in a democracy, as in anything else, you are responsive back to the real power. Felix Rohatyn mentioned that we in business have been notably silent publicly, or inarticulate, when we had the chance to be

William I. Spencer
Citibank of New York

heard in public. On our shoulders rests a great deal of this responsibility.

The appropriateness or the lack of appropriateness of advertising, for instance, is a fantastic thing. How well informed are we? To have the Iranian and the Middle Eastern situation condensed in a minute and a half, and have the directions of our total foreign policy expounded in a minute and a half on the seven o'clock news, is madness. How can we, with the available information at hand, not be better informed of our own all-encompassing well-being? It's a mystery.

I guess that the world is too complicated. If I know just one aspect of our banking business, rather than the entire flow of banking interactions among communities, states, the national government, and in turn, our customers, both corporate and individual, perhaps that's doing pretty well.

It strikes me that somehow, some way, the disasters and near-disasters we're looking at should teach us something. Maybe we've gathered some power from the "Perils of Pauline" undergone by Manhattan and Brooklyn. What we can learn from the Cleveland situation, God knows! Perhaps enough people will sense that we're inevitably sliding; that we *have* slid from the top position in technology, and that words from our government are, unfortunately, lightly regarded in foreign capitals. Perhaps a perception of what our current method of activities is doing to us will alert all of us and prompt us into action, so that we can get something done.

*The topic of partnership among government, business, labor, academia, and the press virtually disappears in a lively discussion of national issues and problems which need fixing.*

*Maybe a basic objective of partnership is already in evidence: a dialogue among people in*

---

"It strikes me that somehow, some way, the disasters and near-disasters we're looking at should teach us something."

*significant positions in American society, holding very different perspectives, is in the process of identifying the most serious problems facing the nation.*

*The general discussion that follows begins in response to a question from the Moderator: Is American business changing its historically apolitical stance?*

### Robert O. Anderson
*Atlantic-Richfield Company*

Obviously, we can't play the role of the paternalistic father of a city; it would be resented, and it wouldn't be proper. But the private sector certainly has responsibility to help support the nonprofit institutions, education and medicine, social activities within our communities, and areas of most direct interest to us.

I wish that we in the private sector had faced this issue many, many years before this, including achieving a somewhat greater level and standard of corporate giving to nonprofit institutions. I don't really know how we are going to get around each other's suspicion.

### Responsibilities of Elected Officials

It's interesting that the political sector is not in much better shape than the private sector. Facing the political sector today is a very real question, on the back of people's minds: Do elected officials have any other responsibility except to get reelected?

The average Congressman has a staff of, say, twenty-five people now, whereas twenty or thirty years ago he might have had a cousin and a secretary working for him. And that cousin wasn't all bad because he really had the Congressman's interest at heart. But now you have a professional crew to open your mail, write your letters, prepare position papers. Anyone who has a staff of twenty to twenty-five people will recognize that it's pretty hard not to end up with your staff doing your thinking. And this goes for any staff, for any position in life.

The public cynicism toward our elected officials stems from the belief that they're literally dedicated only to reelection. This cynical feeling resembles the view that the corporate chief executive has only one interest, and that's to make money. I think we overlook, in looking at corporate people today, that practically all of them are professional people. They're hired hands, whether they're the boss or the guy in the mail room. Everyone today in the large corporations is an employee in almost the full sense of the word. But somehow or other, this suspicion, this hostility, the assumption that the other side is wrong before you even explain the facts, is really an eroding force in our society.

## Energy and Public Attitudes

In the energy situation, we've gone through at least ten, probably twenty, years in which any number of people within the energy industry have seen quite clearly the direction we've been moving. But if they said anything about it, it was immediately termed self-serving: "You're just trying to talk this up so it's to your own advantage." And unfortunately the people who still refuse to believe we have an energy crisis do so on the grounds an energy crisis is self-serving and helpful to the energy industry, probably a bunko game.

Unless we can get around this hostility, it's going to be very difficult. Still it is a three- or four-way problem. If we're just government and business, that's one thing. But it's government, business, labor, and academia. And, of course, the press and the media are important factors. But the press and the media will reflect, I think, the feelings of the four sectors if they're well thought out and they're constructive. But how on earth we're going to get rid of this suspicion and sit down and talk in reasonable terms is probably the biggest single problem.

*The Moderator asks Leonard Silk what he thinks about business's and government's concern with lack of trust, and what he thinks about the fact that business and government apparently rely on the media for transmitting their concerns to the public.*

### Leonard Silk
*The New York Times*

I've been sitting here trying to think of what I could say that would really be constructive and unobvious. It's so easy to mouth generalities. From my own perspective, one of the most important things the press can do is play its role more professionally. I'm not going to put the blame on anybody else, but on the press itself. A lot of people will accept the statement, without thinking what the term professional actually means.

### A Professional Press

It is complicated for the press to become more professional. Increasingly, the press itself is regarded as a special interest. By the people who own it and control it, it *is* a special interest, a business. Well over half of all American newspapers today, for example, are owned by chains. Even without the chain ownership of the press, the television networks have become very big business.

If the press is nothing but a business, it's really not going to be very useful to the society. It has to be more than that. It has to be a kind of a *public interest* institution, very much like the academic community. That means that the people who work for newspapers or television stations, or who control the whole news and editorial function of those institutions, have got to be honest, independent, brave, bold, clear, and absolutely free to pursue their consciences and the truth as they can.

All of that makes lovely engravings for the outside of somebody's temple. To do it on a daily basis is one of the hardest things in the world. Because as you do, you make people angry. Felix Rohatyn said that he was skeptical. After my lifetime, I am very skeptical, not just about institutions but about people. People are very cussed, an egotistical, self-seeking lot, generally. Now, that may be an awful apple of discord to throw into this crowd, but it has to be faced. When you pursue your job as a newspaperman, or a newspaper-woman—one can never use the singular gender in our age, thank goodness—you've got to make people unhappy, you've got to be tough. You've got to let the public know what is going on.

We have to do that job, as tough as it is, and as hard as it is sometimes on people who are involved in institutions. Institutions don't exist, they're file cabinets—it's all people out there, individual human beings. Somehow or other the process works, works to the welfare of the country, however hard it is to go along.

Only one reference was made so far to Watergate. I will now make the second reference. It was one of the most embittering things in our country because we stopped discussing issues, and we began to vilify groups. We began to be people who were charged with trying to destroy a President for self-interested purposes. Even if a President brought on a great deal of this himself, the effect was that we began to personify the things we disagreed with and to treat them as evil or as treasonous.

In the process of examining and exposing what was going on, we have made some steps forward. It's a hard thing to do, because the press itself has acquired some kind of a habit, in the process, of being equally unfair to everybody, equally severe on everybody.

It comes back to the professional role of individual persons in the press, in the academic world, and in all the other institutions: To be fair, to be honest, and at the same time to view our neighbors as people as decent as we are until proven otherwise.


*The Moderator questions the professionalism of the regional newspapers' treatment of business in this country.*

### Leonard Silk
*The New York Times*

I agree that, at the regional level, the business press isn't thoroughly professional. I don't know that it is true for a good deal of the national press.

Incidentally, I have to say, since it's not mine, that television is dreadful in this respect. It's the time constraint that makes it so bad. There's very little you can hear, very little time for analysis.

Daily papers, including *The New York Times* and *The Wall Street Journal*, and increasingly other papers like *The Los Angeles Times*, do a pretty good job.

We've got an awfully good magazine press, including *Business Week*, where I once lived, but also *Fortune* and *U.S. News* and *Forbes*, and so on. Things do get aired and analyzed and kicked around. It may not be as good as our sports coverage in America, but I think it's been improving.

### W. Donham Crawford
*Gulf States Utility Company*

We've been talking about the distrust between business and government, but we're talking primarily about government on the federal level. If everybody else's business is like ours, I think we have much less dissension at the local and state level. Our company serves in Texas and Louisiana, and we really don't find distrustful relationships at state and local governmental levels. We're able to work closely with them, I think, to the common good. It's when you get to the national level problems really begin to bloom in earnest. I suppose that calls for the third reference to Watergate. Watergate, after all, was a national event; that may account for the underlying mood of distrustfulness so distressing to us all. But it does not exist at lower levels of government.

### Douglas Costle
*Environmental Protection Agency*

Basically I disagree with that. I don't think people disaggregate their frustrations with government by level of government. You can get just as frustrated having to spend four hours getting a dog license in Fairfax, Virginia, because they won't accept a Connecticut vaccination certificate. I think it is in a way easier to lob a long distance artillery shell in the direction of Washington because they are a bit further away.

When you begin to look at something like energy, one of the basic problems is that there is no fundamental agreement of what the basic energy facts are. Nobody is willing right now to trust the other fellow's facts. Bob Anderson referred to this earlier. If you don't have a basic agreement on what the energy facts are, how in the world do you fabricate a national policy?

We've been doing an analysis lately of federal permits for new energy facilities. We started in the area of coal-fired power plants. We set up a system whereby we track every single permit application once it is filed with the federal government. Now, we've been told by the energy industry that it takes eight years from the time you decide you want to build a coal-fired power plant until the time you actually turn a shovel of earth. We're tracking a series of these things right through the system to find out how long it takes, and what stops the process along the way. We have in mind a simultaneous review in cases where multiple permits are required so that you don't have an unnecessarily elongated serial process.

It turns out the federal performance on these is not bad. It takes generally less than a year to get those problems worked out. At the Environmental Protection Agency it takes less than five months. There are a lot of loose facts thrown around and allegations, tending to further deepen the mistrust people have. I think we've got to be really quite careful about that. I hear a lot of antiregulatory rhetoric today. The fact of the matter is, we can't afford not to regulate. There are legitimate problems, real problems concerning the manner in which we do that job. The way we do that job has to be much improved, and it can be much improved.

But right now there is a cocoon of rhetoric around this

issue. Frankly, it just simply doesn't square with the facts when you begin to get down to the facts. So I think when you get back to the question of credibility it begins with being more honest with each other and with everybody as to what the facts really are.

## W. Donham Crawford
*Gulf States Utility Company*

This is not an EPA-electric utility industry battle here. We're really talking about government overall—something very, very difficult to understand. Let's look at an example: The National Energy Act, which passed last year, calls, as it should, for industry and utilities to move to coal and nuclear and away from oil and gas. The Department of Energy is now preparing the regulations to implement the Act. We are moving away from oil and gas in our company. We have one last oil-fired unit, Sabine No. 5, being built in East Texas. It's been under construction for several years. It will start into operation on November 1 of this year. We have been put on the "hit list" by the Department of Energy along with fifty-nine other utility companies. The basis for this, as we understand it, is that since that oil-fired unit was not completed in April of 1977, the President first presented his energy proposal to Congress, it's defined as a "new" unit. Now we must prove to the Department of Energy that the unit should not burn coal. You understand, the boiler is sitting there prepared to burn oil, there's no coal there, no railroad tracks, or anything like that, but now we have to go through a regulatory procedure to demonstrate that we shouldn't burn coal. I don't want to go on any more with the example, because it takes too much time, but I submit to you that this is out of control.

## William I. Spencer
*Citibank of New York*

This group is concerned with how we get a partnership. I don't think more dramatic examples of what we perceive to be the other guy's problems is going to add much. Clearly, the question is how do we go about getting a partnership? I come back to where I was before. Are we not facing emergencies in enough areas so that the kinds of things Felix Rohatyn was talking about are indeed a rationale for joining some governors and private enterprises together? Are we not close enough to going down the drain, or to appreciating that we are, to get people together by pointing out what's happening? I don't know. It would be nice if we had some statesmen instead of politicians in office. I think that would help a great deal.

*At this juncture in the first panel discussion, concerning rationale for partnership, the Moderator urges the audience to participate in the discussion. The audience-participation session begins with an explicit question on a specific problem.*

## From the Audience

What is the way to keep politicians from having to run constantly around the clock? Because you're right. No sooner do you get the vacuum cleaner run over you from collections, than you have to go to the testimonial dinner, and the bipartisan thank-you, and so forth. Is it public financing of campaigns? Is it putting a limit on terms? Do you have any ideas that would help?

## Robert O. Anderson
*Atlantic-Richfield Company*

First of all, I would say two-year terms should be revoked. They're ridiculous. A two-year term is simply a permanent campaign. Longer terms, maybe some limit on tenureship—but something that takes the pressure off trying to turn with every gust of wind. If politicians really believed their only responsibility is to get reelected they would have a very easy time in office. All they'd have to do is try to climb on any popular bandwagon that went by and make the necessary number of chicken lunches and dinners. And get staffs that are totally organized toward getting them reelected. I think we are building a gigantic reelection machine, and the two-year term is just an invitation for it.

I've been sitting here thinking of why we have an alienated society, and the alienation toward government and industry. We have a nation that has been, in the last twenty years, more preoccupied with the idea that *you're* number one, that your real interest in life is taking care of yourself, and you should come first. Well, if you really believed that, you would then begin to assume everybody else is only motivated by self-interest. If you believe that, you obviously believe that there aren't any people out there that are any good: in business, in government, or anywhere else. The country has been built on volunteerism. There are a lot of people, thank God, in this country who really are motivated beyond their personal interests. I can't imagine anyone in my industry with any integrity or depth who doesn't realize that the energy problem is bigger than his job. I have said repeatedly, if we in the energy business think we have a problem, if the problem we see happens, the people—our customers—are going to be infinitely more adversely affected by it than we are.

When people serve on government committees, volunteer things, and what-not, they leave their personal interests at home. Think of the people we've had in government service on a voluntary basis in any number of roles. I don't know any of them who carry their own biases and prejudices and personal interests with them. They genuinely try to act in the public good.

**Leonard Silk**
*The New York Times*

We can sometimes go too far in thinking that somehow or other the electorate is right in what it thinks, and that what we have to do is figure out a way to please it. I wish in many ways, as a good admirer of Abraham Lincoln and all that, that that were always so. But we've got an awful lot of ignorant people in the country who are always looking for somebody to blame for everything that goes wrong.

The problem we're talking about is not peculiar to the United States. It exists throughout the Western World, throughout the whole developing world—everywhere. What we have are some terrible problems. They are the problems, if you like, in our part of the world, the industrial world, of late capitalism, of post industrialism. Industrialism hasn't even solved the old problems. Now conflicting interests and objectives are all over the place. They tend, as a result of particular people's desires, to spill out in different problems.

Some we've already referred to, including inflation and the energy problem. These problems aren't just a consequence of dumb bureaucrats. People want different things. They want a tank full of gas any time they want it, and they want cheap electricity whenever they want it, and they want clean air wherever they live. And they don't want plant sites in their backyards if they think they're going to blow up, whether they will or not. And they want low prices, and they want lots of energy. These pressures exist, and are felt in the Congress, and the Congress does have to get reelected all the time.

There are many unsolved problems, in our country and in other countries. People like ourselves, meaning this very elitist gathering in a very populist state and country, have to find the right answers to the problems. Once we do, we have to sell them to the nation, to deliver solutions to the real problems. Then people will settle down again.

There's not been any steady state of public distrust of government. When things went well for awhile, like in the 1950s, everybody registered great confidence not only in government but in business, education, and the press. As everything goes wrong, everybody tends to personify all this, and they say, "I don't trust him; I don't trust her; I don't trust you; I don't trust me." They're looking for somebody to convict. We're in a secular age. You don't think of blaming divine creatures or divine retribution, so you look around for somebody you think has some power, and you say, "It's him, the dumb, selfish bastard!" The problems themselves are the root of the trouble, rather than just human cussedness.

*The Moderator points out that business has already joined hands with government by backing particular candidates, and that Political Action Committees provide a means for business to influence government in areas business knows about: economic viability, productivity, the creation of wealth in private sources and its transfer to public sources of distribution. He asks for comments from the panel.*

### Douglas Costle
*Environmental Protection Agency*

I am treading in water over my head at this point. I understand that the number of Political Action Committees has gone from some small number of eighteen or twenty—I don't know if these numbers are right—to now something closer to two thousand. Put that together with the fact that more money was spent in seven Senatorial races last year than was spent in the Presidential campaign we just came through.

The Political Action Committees will certainly bring new activity to the political arena and to the political campaigns and to Congressional debate over legislation. But I suggest, if the Political Action Committees simply become a way to lobby for a narrow perspective, or a perspective that will in the public mind be viewed as purely partisan self-interest, then the business community in this country may do itself far greater damage than has ever been done in the past. Because I sense that the American public will react dramatically to the thought that a particular sector of our society is able to buy—and it will be characterized that way, fairly or unfairly, right or wrong—that a particular sector of society is attempting to buy its own perspective by buying the government. Such a public reaction could be very dangerous.

I don't know what the answer is. I'm far from convinced that public financing of elections is the answer. I see just as many problems there; it's a dilemma.

*The Moderator observes that public trust in the partnership must follow after the partners themselves come to some agreement. He asks the panel how they think the partnership can get started, considering where we are now. No academician, for instance, can be appointed to the Department of Energy if he or she has ever been a consultant to, or even worked for, an oil or utility company.*

## W. Donham Crawford
*Gulf States Utility Company*

It seems to me the first thing you have to have is the determination of both sides to make it succeed. I believe business would like to have a closer, more constructive, less distrustful relationship with the government, and would be prepared to do anything reasonable toward that end. I suspect that the government, on the other hand, would feel pretty much the same way, but may not feel that it has the freedom to do so, particularly in the light of recent events. But if the government could bring itself to try new approaches to develop the relationship, that is the first requisite.

If there were a joint determination to form a partnership, perhaps a way to start is just to start: to have some particular event or circumstance or problem addressed jointly, and use that as a demonstration.

## Leonard Silk
*The New York Times*

I would like to reiterate one thing that has already been stated, at least implicitly, by Felix Rohatyn. In the old days you had partnerships because most people weren't looking or didn't care; you had, in effect, an establishment, or whatever you call it, that ran things. I think that that doesn't work anymore. I think that to have an effective business-government-labor partnership nowadays, you've got to be prepared to be open. You've got to let the public know what you are doing. It will trust you if it can see you and hear you, and if what you say makes sense.

If I can just underline what Felix Rohatyn said, that was really the story in New York, whether it was Felix's own personal insight or somebody else's or several people's. They did have enough sense to bring the press in, to bring the public in, to say, "Here we are, if you want to ask us any questions, fine, this is what we're doing, this Vicky Gottbaum from the Municipal Workers, and this is Walt Wriston, the well-known scoundrel from Citibank." And that's the way it has to be done. But I don't mean show, I don't mean P.R., I mean really let them know, really talk it over, really say what the options are.

I happen to think that this applies to the Federal Reserve Board—God forbid, as far as some bankers are concerned. This is not to say that every single thing, every decision, every dream you have must immediately be exposed on color television while you're having it. But you know what I mean, without trying to define it too closely. We've got to be open, or the people will distrust us, and maybe properly.

**Robert O. Anderson**
*Atlantic-Richfield Company*

I think that the influence of Political Action Committees can never be great because the limitations on individual giving are quite strict. I think anyone would be naive to think for two hundred dollars you're going to buy a Congressman or Senator. Fortunately that is not true. You don't. It's illegal. The thousand dollar maximum contribution limitation has stopped abuses in buying somebody. But as a practical matter, there is very little of that in recent years at the national level.

We have something far more interesting in our company: a civic action program, started a few years ago. We simply wrote our shareholders and our employees and said, "If you would like to be advised of legislation and matters that affect your company, your job, we will make you a member of our Civic Action Program, and we'll mail you information that we think you should have if you're an interested owner or employee or retiree." We have 55,000 people in the program now—a potentially more powerful influence than the modest amount of money that comes out of our Political Action Committee. Fifty-five thousand people writing letters are a significant force. We do not tell them how to write; we just explain what the issue is, the pros and cons, and how it might affect their company.

But it indicates two things. One, that 55,000 people are interested enough to write back and say, "Yes, I'd like to do it."

In one case a Congressman's office called our office in Washington and said, "What was the number of that bill that you people in Maryland have been writing us about?" So it means somebody is getting through to the mail.

Now, you can buy elected officials with votes but you can't buy them with money. But if you can deliver votes—everybody knows, in this elective system, you can get influence with votes. But you're not going to get it with the kind of money that's under the new regulations, which are good.

*The panelists agree that not only is business responsive to the market, but government, too, is answerable: to the voters. Both business and government are dependent on the people. On this note, the discussion shifts. A leading question from the audience results in a thoughtful scrutiny of just who decides crucial issues in this country—such as how much and in what way we are going to develop nuclear power. How the American decisionmaking process differs from that in Europe is also mentioned.*

## From the Audience:

Why is it that other countries can put up their nuclear reactors, and they are, while we are having such a rough time?

**Douglas Costle**
*Environmental Protection Agency*

Prior to my going to Washington to be head of EPA, I was the Environmental Commissioner for the State of Connecticut. The principal power company in Connecticut, Northeast Utilities, is now fifty percent nuclear. The basic problem we always had in licensing nuclear power plants was the siting question: Where do you put it? What does it do to the surrounding environment? For the most part, we were able to resolve those questions.

A study was done a few years back that looked at the delays in the construction of nuclear power plants to ask: Why do we increasingly have these delays? It turned out that of six or seven years' worth of delays, only a fraction had to do with environmental questions. Most had to do with the fact that these are all designed and built as unique one-of-a-kinds, so they always come up with their own set of problems. Maybe engineering design or construction; or it may be faulty materials; it may be weather; it can be a whole range of things. But I was surprised to find out that environmental delays were not a significant fraction of the total time involved in trying to get a plant built.

Nuclear power is in fact very controversial in this country, for a couple of reasons. One is that the public is uneasy about what the facts are. They get confusing new data seemingly each month that goes by. We have submitted the bill that was designed to try to expedite that process by which nuclear power plants get permitted. The basic permitting is increasingly consolidated in a single agency, the Nuclear Regulatory Agency.

With respect to conventional power, the big problem is public acceptance. The minute you try to build, it's a little like trying to locate a garbage dump. Everyone knows we need it, we want it, but "not in my backyard, for Pete's sake." And the legal process does give people an opportunity to weigh in and be heard on that subject, and that can extend the length of time it takes to get a decision made.

The basic problem with nuclear power is that we have

not solved the question of what to do with nuclear waste. I think the federal government has fallen down in its responsibility of offering a credible solution, even on an interim basis. A major effort is going on within the Administration right now to propose a credible solution to nuclear waste.

There is a whole range of other issues raised in the question of the breeder reactor—the whole notion of a plutonium economy. It's a very subtle set of issues that have troubling implications in terms of how our society functions. These issues simply haven't been thought through to the point where you can achieve a national consensus saying, "Yes, go ahead and do that."

Certainly in Western Europe they're having an increasingly difficult time in licensing nuclear power facilities. They had a big dispute in Sweden, and one in England, over the reprocessing facility and the idea of the first breeder reactor. In the international forum in which I participate, the question my colleagues in Western Europe ask is: "Can you tell us something about how you manage citizen participation, because our people are nervous and upset, and they're protesting and they're barricading these plant sites?"

I suspect that some of the concerns that we've been experiencing are happening, perhaps belatedly, in Europe; but they are certainly beginning to happen. Now, their traditions over there in terms of the citizen's role vis-à-vis the government is quite different from ours. So it may play out in an entirely different way. There is an undeniable public skepticism about nuclear power which we have not been able to satisfy in the public mind.

My own view on conventional nuclear plants is that we need them; we've designed them to be remarkably safe. The probability of an incident is virtually negligible. We have not, in my judgment, solved the waste problem, and that's a serious problem. The federal government has to take preemptive action there if that's to be done—even if it includes, in the near term, custodial responsibility as we search for a longer term solution.

## Robert O. Anderson
*Atlantic-Richfield Company*

The real misfortune is that we are not prepared to build nuclear plants, apparently because of public opinion. But it is the real hope for low cost energy, the only option that can bring us energy at reasonable prices. Everything has a risk. If I had to live near a large generating plant, and could choose between living near a nuclear plant or a coal-fired plant, I'd choose the nuclear plant. I do like to see the sky, and it's quiet, and it would be my own risk evaluation. We do have definite risks from coal-fired or fossil fuels: particulate matter going into the atmosphere. We really don't know what we're doing, long range, to world climate, but we know we're not helping it. So the particulate matter and the $CO_2$ could be a much greater problem than some risk of radiation. As I said earlier today, we've got to learn to live with risks. We take risks every time we get in the car.

## W. Donham Crawford
*Gulf States Utility Company*

I would agree with Mr. Costle about the relatively small part of the very long delays being attributable to environmental factors. But whatever the cause, while some countries can build nuclear plants in five or six years (and I agree that they are beginning to have some problems), ours take ten to twelve years. While Connecticut has fifty percent and Chicago has fifty or sixty percent, as a nation only eleven to twelve percent of our electric power output is nuclear.

If we could increase that, we could hold down the oil imports, thus helping our balance of payments problems, strengthening our dollar, and all the rest. The thing that is needed to further the cause of nuclear power and permit us to go ahead and use it is a strong, articulate, forcefully communicated message from the President of the United States. And we have not had that. The public sees Mr. Carter's policy on nuclear as equivocal because of his statements during the campaign. He changed those; both he and Dr. Schlesinger have said that we must rely on light-water reactors, and indeed we must.

But he has never really gotten it across to the public. I submit that if the President would say, "Well, maybe I don't like it, but we've got to have it in the national interest," and persuade the public that he's for it, and then at the same time have the federal government (in whatever ways are available short of legislation) streamline the processes, we'd get on with the job of nuclear, to the great benefit of the country.

**From the Audience:**

There have been moods afoot lately, especially in the Securities and Exchange Commission, to restrict the flow of people from government back to industry. What sort of problems do you think this may cause? Is there a more realistic way to handle the problems and yet avoid the obvious potential conflict of interest that arises with that?

**William I. Spencer**
*Citibank of New York*

I don't perceive this to be a great problem. It was mentioned earlier in relation to our current perception of what is right and wrong, that anybody who had ever had anything to do with the energy business couldn't get a job having anything to do with the regulation of energy. So, anyone that knows anything about anything can't get exposed or be a part of a regulatory operation in government.

I feel it is a terrible tragedy to assume that anybody who knows the energy business is automatically going to be prejudiced. Exactly the same thing is true of the perception that it is very bad for somebody who has been in the Federal Reserve to be precluded from going back into the banking business. So what? All the regulations are applicable to them, as they are to everybody else in the business.

**Douglas Costle**
*Environmental Protection Agency*

I'm not an expert on ethics legislation, but a bill that did go through—whistled through the Congress, just like that—

is now causing people some considerable concern. I don't think anybody thought the whole thing through to the end of the sentence. What I think is surprising is that when you look at all the public opinion polls, one of the most frequently cited reasons for distrust of the government is the appearance of a kind of an incestuous relationship between regulators and those whom they regulate. Regulators have frequently come from the business communities which they are then expected to regulate.

People aren't really sure what that means, but it worries them. The fact of the matter is, you find a revolving door. But a corrupt public official is one of the rarest birds in this country. It is amazing, in fact, how responsible and honest the bulk of our public officials are, given what we normally pay them, including those we elect.

I don't think we've found the right answer. The new ethics legislation, in my own personal judgment, is not necessarily the right answer. But it was almost inevitable you would see legislation like that, given the underlying lack of credibility and concern on the part of the public about the nature of this *in fact* existing partnership or relationship between government and business.

**Leonard Silk**
*The New York Times*

It's a very hard thing to deal with, but there are ways of limiting the areas where people have a right to be concerned. If you take somebody who, say, has served in the Pentagon in a procurement job, and then shifts over to a defense contractor, dealing with precisely the same people who were working for him, and so on, he is in an advantageous position over somebody else. This is unfair. This is an example of what President Eisenhower termed the industrial-defense complex in operation.

There are some situations analagous to that in other agencies of government, whether defense or nondefense, whether regulatory or nonregulatory. I'm not sure, not being a lawyer or whatever, exactly how you go about monitoring this problem. But I don't think it's a matter of, for example, taking an economist who's been working as an adviser to the Federal Reserve Board, and saying he dare not work for a private bank. That's a very different situation from taking somebody who has been on the buying side one day and is on the selling side the next day. You need some regulations, laws, that specify what sort of jobs in the private sector a person may hold or may not hold after holding a government job—at least for a period of time, say five years.

# III Priorities for Partnership

Introduction: **Robert Strauss,**
Special Representative for
Trade Negotiations

Moderator: **Ben Love,**
Chief Executive Officer,
Texas Commerce Bancshares, Inc.

Panelists: **Jack Conway,**
Senior Vice President,
United Way of America

**William Coors,**
Chairman of the Board,
Adolph Coors Company

**John Swearingen,**
Chairman,
Standard Oil Co. of Indiana

# Summary: Priorities for Partnership

We seem to be entering a new era of partnership among government, business, labor, and academia. A different kind of attitude and understanding is emerging, one that seemed remote twenty-five years ago. Most of the panel, following the lead of the speaker, Bob Strauss, agree that cooperation must replace confrontation if we're to solve national problems. But nearly everyone also voices reservations.

The kind of partnership we're talking about is discussed. If business and labor become partners with government, who will be the senior partner and who the junior partner? Is equal partnership possible? The nature and necessity of partnership is probed, and the priorities facing such a partnership are enumerated. Energy, inflation, trade, and unemployment are cited as chief priorities.

Correcting public misconceptions concerning the functioning of our economic system and sorting out the government regulatory situation are other priorities debated. The cost of regulation is seen as a major problem, but not an impossible barrier, to partnership. Dealing with excessive regulation seems to offer an incentive to forging a partnership.

The prevalence throughout history of the revolt against oppressive government is mentioned in connection with the central tenet of liberty in American life, prefatory to discussing the possibility of replacing government control with more cooperative means of achieving social goals.

The panel does not reach a consensus on just the right degree of coalition that is needed among the various sectors in order to solve national problems, or decide on exactly how much the traditional adversarial relationship protects the people in a free society. It is agreed, however, that ways must be found to structure the very real problems we face in such a way that we can agree on objectives and on the trade-offs needed to even begin to solve them. Again, such structuring of the problems facing the nation, it is agreed, depends on consensus concerning issues and approaches.

Achieving some degree of cooperation among traditionally disparate sectors appears to be a job, an assignment, the panelists are willing to take on.

# III Priorities for Partnership

**Robert Strauss**
*Special Representative for
Trade Negotiations*

*Ambassador Robert Strauss graduated from the University
of Texas Law School in 1941. After brief service as an F.B.I.
agent, he founded his own law firm in Dallas in 1946. He has
served on the boards of such companies as Xerox Corporation, Braniff Airways, Columbia Pictures, and the Wylain
Corporation. He was elected treasurer of the Democratic
National Convention in 1970; in 1972 he assumed chairman-
ship of that convention. As Special Representative for Trade
Negotiations, Ambassador Strauss's accomplishments
include convincing steel companies to roll back prices and
improving United States trade agreements with Japan.*

## The Interdependent Economic World

In Stamford, Texas, where I lived when I first came
here, economic life was really very simple. If we had good
rains around the square, within a few miles of the square the
cotton grew; and if the boll weevils didn't get it and the price
was halfway decent, we had what they called a good year. A
good year meant that the farmers had a little cash and they
paid the banks and paid the merchants; before they went
back in debt, and the whole town lived a little better for the

next few months. We all thought we were prospering, and it all depended upon whether or not it rained.

I left Stamford and I came here for an education. It's been a long and constant learning process. I've learned that the economic health of this country has grown exceedingly complicated and delicate, and dependent upon many factors, both domestic and international. Time and progress have certainly reduced the two hundred miles from here to Stamford that impressed me as being such a great distance.

I've learned since that time that actions taking place in Bonn or in Peking or Paris or Moscow can affect life not only in the great capitals of the world, but also in Stamford, Texas just as dramatically and just as quickly as does the rain that falls or doesn't fall around the square.

It's in the context of that kind of interdependent world that I want to touch upon several of the concerns I believe must be the focus of our priorities in the coming years, if we're going to move ahead. I should also like to discuss the crucial issue of international trade that has been my personal responsibility in the Carter Administration.

**Cooperation and Consensus**

In the past, we've often profited by a healthy distance and a healthy scrutiny between the public and the private sectors of our economy. But we may very well be at a point today, where besides trying to get government more and more out of our lives, we are also trying to define some ways for the public and private sectors to pull closer together. More harmony and more cooperation is needed—more partnership—than we have had in the past, or our nation is going to continue to suffer.

The next decade, most likely, will present changes in economic conditions for the nation far larger than most of us think as we move toward it on a day-by-day basis, mainly because the rate of growth during the rest of this century is

---

**"In the past, we've often profited by a healthy distance and a healthy scrutiny between the public and private sectors of our economy."**

going to be slower than past rates have been. Our rapid growth and continued expansion has enabled us to ease a lot of tensions in the past.

When the pie keeps getting larger and larger and larger, as we've seen it do, it's easier to deal with economic and social problems in the short run. But when the pie doesn't get larger, or if it grows at a much slower rate, and demands become not only larger but accelerate, tensions develop that tend to tear us apart.

The central problem we're going to have in this country, in the 1980s, is dealing with tensions between groups and sectors. Slower growth rates will undoubtedly present us with new and difficult economic and social issues, requiring us, as I said, to pull together instead of apart.

We can no longer continue at war with ourselves, intensifying the shrillness that pits interest group against interest group. We're going to have to develop cooperation to replace what has become almost classic confrontation in this country.

And to do that, we're going to have to have involvement on the part of the private sector. We're going to have to make the Ben Loves and the Bill Coorses and the others get far more deeply involved. Not let them become isolated because they don't like politics, or they don't like government, or they fear bad publicity, or unfavorable gossip, or comment from their friends.

President Kennedy was fond of saying, "Our problems are man-made, and therefore they can be solved by man." But it's essential that we move toward a national consensus on some key economic issues. By "national consensus" I mean in terms of thrust, not in terms of the fact that we must march lockstep in agreement.

## Productivity

First, let's recognize together that improving our

---

**"We're going to have to develop cooperation to replace what has become almost classic confrontation in this country."**

productivity is fundamental to increasing our competitive position and the market power that is so essential for the United States.

Many of our respected economists and business leaders have identified deterioration in capital formation as a major contributor to our productivity slump. I certainly agree with them. We've got to try to get that in order and deal with it.

We've got to try to shape, for example, our tax expenditures. I don't know what portion it ought to be, but I do know that we've got to get a maximum of business capital formation per tax dollar. I personally believe (many will disagree) that accelerated depreciation, investment tax credits, and corporate rate cuts, for example, are far more efficient ways of dealing with this problem than are capital gains. I'm not opposed to capital gains; they have a role. I just think we get more "bang for the buck" in some of these other ways.

The President, as many of you know, has established a cabinet-level National Productivity Council to examine some of these issues. This group is aware that the decrease in both public and private funds devoted to research has promoted a fall-off in the innovation that we desperately need.

The proper government response to the question of productivity isn't very clear. It isn't to me, and I serve on that board. Do we try to stimulate greater research and development through tax incentives? Or do we target funds to help one industry, moving ahead more quickly and getting more for the dollar? Or do we go into another industry in another area because the need is greater? I don't know the answer to that.

And to raise another key question, just what are the budgetary priorities in this time of the budget-cutting and the budget-balancing that we need so desperately? Cut his or her program, not mine. That's the priority. Don't cut mine, cut yours!

I've dealt with every constituency in this country while trying to put together a trade package. We surely know that every sector in this economy is after theirs. Very rarely does the phone ever ring and someone say, "Bob, I want to tell you what I think the national interest is." It's always, "Let me tell you why I need mine." We all do the same thing.

## Government Regulation

Let's also consider the impact and the desirability of further government regulation. We're all aware of the advantages of clean air and clean water. I certainly want them for my children and grandchildren. We all want safe products, decent working conditions, and a better quality of life.

But where does the regulation begin and where does it stop, and what do all of our regulations do to our productivity? The Council on Wage and Price Stability estimates that our government regulation is probably ten percent of our current inflation. Is that too much? Is that too little? I don't know.

President Carter's commitment to a healthy and safe environment is very strong. But his Administration has begun to reverse the process of unquestioning growth in federal regulations. New regulations are issued only when needed, and they must meet their approved goals at the lowest possible cost.

But you never read about that. They testified on the Hill with respect to some regulatory controls, the first of the week—it was a great controversy, because it seemed as if we were tearing down all of the regulatory efforts of the past decade. It wasn't true. They were trying to put some cost analysis into a number of regulations; this particular testimony was with respect to the environment.

Fascinating! We hear all the criticism about regulations. I inquired at the White House in *favor* of the testimony. I wonder how many wires they receive in criticism of the regulations. So we've got to get involved. Someone has to

---

**"Just what are the budgetary priorities in this time of the budget-cutting and the budget-balancing that we need so desperately? Cut his or her program, not mine. That's the priority."**

care and someone has to be heard. Concern with overregulation is just part and parcel of the fight we must make with respect to inflation.

People today want and need and demand less governmental intrusion in their lives. Not more. People reject mandatory controls; they prefer a voluntary program relying heavily on the common sense and cooperation of both business and labor. The program has many imperfections, but we're trying hard to make it work.

We rarely see involvement in terms of the two-thirds of the glass that's full, that's positive and good. We only see the one-third of the program that isn't working, or doesn't work, or has its imperfections. We need more involvement, more cooperation, and less confrontation.

I hardly need point out that we must continue to work for a more sound and coherent energy policy. Although what this Administration has done leaves much to be desired, major steps have been made in the right direction. But I'll leave the energy question to others here more competent to discuss it than I am. Let me talk about trade.

**Trade**

There are those among you who would counsel that the way to answer our terrible problems of trade deficits today is to close the door, put a fence around the country, and stop foreign imports.

Well, we tried that once, in the early '30s. A fellow named Smoot and a fellow named Hawley wrote a bill called Smoot-Hawley; it was the most protectionist piece of legislation this nation has ever seen. It had a great impact. Probably more than any other factor, the Smoot-Hawley Bill changed a recession into a major worldwide depression that took its toll in tragedy the likes of none we've ever seen before.

World trade today is just simply too big to ignore. We can't expect world trade to go away. We can't be foolish about it. Bismarck once commented that "God holds His hand quite particularly over fools, and drunkards, and the United States of America." With our abundance of natural resources, technology, capital, and an ever-expanding domestic market, of course we've been able to be foolish, or at least not wise, and still do well. But now we're faced with an altogether different set of circumstances.

We're faced with a near-term necessity; we've seen large oil imports and a major balance-of-payments gap. We've got to develop some export capacity.

I've seen what the Japanese and the Germans, and others, have done while *not* involving government in business affairs. Even in Japan, although people think they have, they really haven't done that. But they *do* have government cooperation; the government and the private sector have cooperated in many respects.

Just think, for example, that only a few years ago Japan really had no computer capability. Today, they compete on almost an equal basis with our own computer companies. Just a handful of years. It's my judgment, that before the middle 1980s, you're going to see the same thing in aircraft, where we now dominate the world. We're not going to be able to do that any more.

So, instead of turning back the clock, we'd better look forward. What we're trying to do in Geneva—we've got some ninety nations involved—is to negotiate, and bring into being, a new set of trading rules.

A set of trading rules: it's hard to believe that for generations, men and women such as yourselves, and nations such as ours, have been going to the trading tables of the world, acquiring tremendous amounts of knowledge and a lot of experience, but there has never been written and recorded a set of up-to-date rules to guide the game of trade. That's what we're trying to do now in Geneva.

A lot of barnacles have grown up. We're not engaged just in a tariff exercise, but we're negotiating, firm and hard, on

---

**"With our abundance of natural resources, technology, capital, and an ever-expanding domestic market, of course we've been able to be foolish, or at least not wise, and still do well. But now we're faced with an altogether different set of circumstances."**

the difficult job of trying to lower tariffs a bit. Far more importantly, we're dealing with nontariff barriers to trade: trying to break down the barriers that prevent our people from having the same kind of access to foreign markets as they have to ours.

We're trying to see that the standards are the same, so that a different standard of product in a foreign company doesn't keep our product out. We're trying to insure that licensing is done according to common rules. Any foreign nation, any foreign company, can bid on a government job in our country. It makes it more competitive. In foreign lands we don't have that opportunity. We need fair access to foreign markets.

We'll open some 25 billions of dollars of possible business a year for American concerns to bid on. We're getting into the question of foreign subsidies, so our Texas oranges don't have to compete in foreign country "A" with oranges shipped in from foreign country "B" that are subsidized by the government. Our Valley farmer here in Texas doesn't get any such help.

We're coming to grips with export subsidies. I could go on and on with the subjects that we're covering. Customs evaluation is another very complicated thing. But what we're about is not going to change the trade balance of this world.

It's just the beginning. It's the first two or three chapters in a long, long book called trade. But it needs to be done. I would hope that each of you would examine our work product over the next few weeks. I hope to complete it in the next month or so and present it to the Congress and try my darndest to pass it. I think you're going to find that it's a good product.

I spoke of the one-third and two-thirds glass, and if you look only at the one-third of the things that we didn't accomplish there's no way in the world you could support it.

---

**"There has never been written and recorded a set of up-to-date rules to guide the game of trade. That's what we're trying to do now in Geneva."**

If you look at the two-thirds of the glass that's full—
what this nation has accomplished—then you can't fail to
support this trade package. Because the world will be a better
place to trade for American products and American
produce, and markets will be more accessible, if we complete
this negotiation and get the Congress to approve it.

We have a lot to do in this country. Walter Lippman
wrote some words about forty years ago, before this nation
went to war, more applicable today than they were the day he
wrote them:

> You took the good things for granted, and now you
> must earn them again. It is written that for every right
> that you cherish you have a duty which you must fulfill.
> And for every hope you entertain for you and for yours
> you have a duty you ought to try to fulfill, and you have
> a task you must perform. And for every good that you
> wish could happen, you will have to sacrifice just a bit of
> your comfort and ease.

My friends, in 1979, there is nothing for nothing in America
anymore.

**Ben Love**
*Chief Executive Officer,*
Texas Commerce
Bancshares, Inc.

*Ben Love is a banker: Chairman, President, and Chief Executive Officer of Texas Commerce Bancshares, Inc. He serves on the Board of Directors of the International Monetary Fund and on the boards of a number of industries, including Proler International Corporation, Hughes Tool Company, Cox Broadcasting Corporation, A.P.S., Inc., and Big 3 Industries. He is a cultural leader of his home city of Houston and a graduate of The University of Texas at Austin, of which he was designated a Distinguished Alumnus.*

## Beginning a New Era

Another era seems to have come into being in the last two years. Before we consider this new mood, let's talk about the first era. Bob Strauss mentioned the importance of trade: this country's protectionist policy and protectionist legislation, if it did not trigger, certainly accelerated, the plunge into a worldwide depression.

From the 1930s on, through maybe 1978, unemployment and how to cure it was the number-one cry in political party after political party, race after race. But about 1978 the unemployment question began to subside. Creeping up into top priority appeared another problem, consistently addressed by every political aspirant: inflation.

Gone are the times of skeptics about the number of jobs this country can produce. Many of you will remember that when Henry Wallace was Vice President, there were many across the country who thought he was very foolish. That lingering doubt was totally dispelled, and they *knew* he was crazy, when he wrote the book *Sixty Million Jobs.* Because that was an impossibility. Now we have ninety-three million people, more or less, working in this country. The job priority might be in the second or third place today.

As Bob Strauss has identified the problems, we have inflation and regulation uppermost in our minds. This panel might talk about what Bob centered on: what's right, rather than what's wrong, and what should we do?

John Swearingen startled me when he said to me earlier that we've got to work with government. John Swearingen hasn't always spoken precisely those words. He has been the champion of business in the role of adversary to the government.

I think most of us envision that when businessmen talk together, the chief subject is excessive, destructive regulation from the federal government. Certainly that's a priority today.

**Capital Formation**

Capital formation in this country, mentioned earlier, is an important but distressing element to consider when identifying the priorities of business and government. We are, in terms of creating capital essential to plant investment, saving about fourteen percent of our GNP for that kind of investment. Japan is saving thirty-two percent of its GNP in the capital formation structure.

We had, in the period of time dating from about 1962 through 1976, an average increase in our annual productivity of about 2.6 percent. Last year it was .4 percent. We have a serious problem with production and a serious problem with our failure to contribute a sufficient percentage of our GNP to capital formation for new plants and equipment.

Bob Strauss set the keynote. A couple of years ago, when he talked about what we should be addressing today, he talked about the politician. But Bob defined the politician a little differently than he did today. Then he described a politician as the man who seeks money from the rich, who seeks votes from the poor, and in the process promises each to save the one from the other.

I think we need consistency. I think we need honesty. I think we need to work together to where we are open and can trust one another. We have the kind of panel that can identify the priorities for a business-labor-government partnership.

*Each speaker in the following panel discussion presents a lucid and consistent view. Jack Conway comes close to expressing areas of common accord, and provides a summary of the priority problems facing the nation. He shows the importance of defining and structuring the problems facing us by clearly identifying objectives, and joins in the discussion on the costs of implementing decisions.*

*The notion of cost, and of varying degrees of cost depending on how far a decision is carried out, becomes a fundamental part of the ongoing debate of the symposium.*

*William Coors discusses the costs of regulating business. He also brings up some of the underlying assumptions of the free enterprise system and argues that the American people are ignorant of how the system works. John Swearingen reminds us of the key American concepts of liberty and responsibility before he too turns to the nagging problem of regulation.*

**Jack T. Conway**
*Senior Vice President,*
United Way of America

*Jack Conway is currently Senior Vice President of United Way
of America in charge of government and labor relations.
Before that he was Executive Director of the American
Federation of State, County and Municipal Employees. In
1965 he was a presidential appointee to the Office of Economic
Opportunity. Mr. Conway has also served as Executive
Director of the Industrial Union Department, AFL-CIO
(1963-1968), and as President of Common Cause (1971-1975),
among the most active lobby groups in Washington. He has
worked through most of his career in the labor movement; for
twenty-four years he was a labor union official in the United
Auto Workers Union (UAW).*

## New Structures from Cooperation

When Bob Strauss set Felix Rohatyn up to be drafted by
the Emergency Financial Control Board (a job that kept him
in business for three and a half years), I sat as the executive
director of the largest public employee union in New York
City. We had massive problems: 130,000 members subject to
potential layoff, loss of jobs on a permanent basis, freezing of
benefits, a whole host of things.

We debated, I'd say, two or three months before the crisis
finally hit. We had to decide whether, as an organization, we
should try to save the city, or whether we should go through
the actual bankruptcy proceedings that were the alternative:
an extremely difficult decision on the part of the union.

But we made the correct decision. The decision was to
save the city. To do whatever we could as an organization—

working with the private sector and with government officials many didn't have a very high regard for—to do what could be done to save the city.

It was out of that whole process that these instruments of the Financial Control Board, the Municipal Assistance Corporation, and so on, were fashioned: new instruments for dealing with impossible problems. People are saying that a few years from now New York City will probably be better off than most major cities in the country. Because New Yorkers will have a modern system of accounting for their activities, they will be better able to cope with future problems.

**Priority Problems: Energy, Inflation, Trade, Unemployment**

As a nation we're faced with four problems almost as intractable as those of the City of New York when it was facing bankruptcy. These problems will have to be dealt with in this country. It will require the kind of partnership that we've been talking about.

We need to develop an energy policy that will reduce our dependency on oil from outside our own nation. We've got to face the problems of inflation and resolve them under extremely difficult circumstances. We need for the first time as a nation to realize that we can't run trade deficit year after year, that we've got to evolve some trade policies which will permit us to function in an interdependent world.

We've got to do all of these things at the same time we're holding unemployment down and creating literally millions of new jobs to keep our citizens fully occupied and able to support themselves and their families. This is an almost impossible task, for as you address any *one* of these four priority problem areas, and begin to succeed, you exacerbate the others.

If you develop an energy policy that recognizes that we're shifting from a low-cost energy economy to a high-cost energy economy, and take the appropriate steps to go through the kind of transition needed to free up resources to develop additional energy sources, you are at the same time running directly contrary to the espoused aims of controlling inflation, holding wages down, holding prices down, and so on.

Jack T. Conway
United Way of America

The labor unions face the trade questions with great fear. I've seen the labor movement move from an almost open endorsement of free-trade policy to one that is very close to protectionism. Laboring people in this country have seen their technologies and their jobs exported—exported to nations that we were interested in helping to rebuild after World War II and to some new nations that we were interested in helping to develop.

Our competitors are now Germany, Japan, Hong Kong, Korea, and Taiwan. It's very difficult for union members and union leaders to see things happen which in effect move the technologies from plants in their own communities to other countries. And then to see goods shipped back into this country, presumably for them to buy—without jobs.

It's a very intricate set of problems that can only be resolved by the business community, and the government, and the labor unions effectively working together and educating the citizenry of this country, who are not used to thinking in these terms.

It took the combination of the Steel Workers Union and the steel industry to bring the problem of steel industry imports fully to the attention of this country. It was only then that Bob Strauss was able to begin to get trade issues up on the front burner where people could accept that things were going to be different.

**Trade-offs and Objectives**

These kinds of intractable problems have to be resolved in our country through the types of partnerships that we're talking about. These problems require trade-offs. They require people giving up something and settling for something less than what they think they're entitled to.

These trade-offs can only be accomplished, when you have such disparity of interest, by setting forth some rather clear objectives. Those objectives can be fully supported in a

---

**"As you address any *one* of these four priority problem areas [energy, inflation, trade, unemployment], and begin to succeed, you exacerbate the others."**

political context by the citizenry only when they are clearly formulated national goals held out for people to inspect, and understand, and commit themselves to.

Then the trade-offs make sense. Then the objectives will make sense. Then it's possible to extend the public-private partnership we're talking about into three or four other areas, substantive areas we're going to have to address very quickly.

**Retooling America**

We've got to retool America. We're functioning with obsolete plants and obsolete tools. We'll have to make a major commitment in order to get competitive again. You can only solve your trade problems if you can compete. You can only compete if you've got good tools and good factories, good working conditions, good products—and you want to compete.

We have an attitude problem as well as a retooling problem that we're going to have to face in this country. We've got to revitalize our cities. We've got to rebuild our bridges. We've allowed things to fall into disrepair. There is an enormous amount of work to be done, but we can't get to it because of the pressures. The squeeze is on us in the general economy.

As we see the federal government getting out of the business of providing services to human needs in the country and pushing these responsibilities back to the states and to the local communities, we have to develop new, effective delivery systems to provide these services for people in need. We've been fashioning a public-private partnership in this country for a number of years.

That's what I'm deeply involved in at the present time in the United Way System. If there is anything that you can hold out in the country as an ideal example of a public-private partnership—business, labor, the local communities—it's the United Way System.

---

"You can only compete if you've got good tools and good factories, good working conditions, good products—and you want to compete."

The other thing we've got to do, finally, and this is a question of the *kind* of society we have, is to start thinking again about community. We've got to start thinking again in terms of our families, our neighborhoods, our local communities. We've got to put them together again in a modern sort of way, much as they used to be when they provided all kinds of support systems for people who needed help. We've got to go forward and help each other much in the way we did in the earlier years of our country and our lives.

That's the way I see it. Those are tough priorities and it's going to take a partnership to accomplish them.

**William K. Coors**
*Chief Executive Officer,*
Adolph Coors Company

*William K. Coors, a native of Colorado, graduated from Phillips Exeter Academy before going to Princeton University, where he received both a Bachelor of Science degree and a Master's degree in chemical engineering. He began working for Adolph Coors Company in 1939. Some fifteen years later he became President, and in 1960 Chairman of the Board. In 1977 Joseph Coors, his brother, assumed the presidency; William Coors retains the responsibility of Chairman of the Board and Chief Executive Officer. The Coors Company has long been committed to a total environmental control program.*

## Economic Understanding

As I look at this matter of priorities, I can't see the possibility of a constructive and productive partnership between the public and the private sectors of our society unless there is a philosophical attitude within our society that is compatible to that partnership.

That attitude does not exist today. Our government, of course, is a government of the people. Government policy is determined by the people. A large majority of the people in this society of ours are very negative toward private business, and they are negative for two reasons.

One, abysmal ignorance of our system—no knowledge of it. And two, some gross misconceptions as to how it works.

### Gallup Poll Findings

Let me share with you, for example, the result of a survey

that was conducted out of Princeton for the United States Chamber of Commerce by George Gallup in 1976. The date is somewhat stale, but recent surveys confirm that it is not all that stale. Before I relate the feeling of the person in the street toward American business, keep in mind that our system—we call it "free enterprise"—has one priceless ingredient that is lacking in any other economic system. That ingredient is competition.

And what makes our system function, what makes our system so great, what makes our system one that has carved out the greatest standard of living of any society in the history of the world, is that element of competition. Competition keeps the action reasonable.

The average after-tax take on the corporate dollar in this country, in this great system of the production and distribution of the goods and services that we all need, is less than five percent. It is competition that holds it down. That is the average level at which the private sector is willing to operate. And if somebody does a little bit better, there is always somebody there in a free society to jump in and provide the competition that holds it down.

Now, question: Are you satisfied or dissatisfied with our American free-enterprise system? Sixty-eight percent of the people asked said they were dissatisfied.

What is the average net after-tax profit to American corporations on their sales? Consensus, thirty-three percent—about seven times more than it actually was.

Question: What would you consider to be an acceptable level of profit? Answer: Seventeen percent.

Now, that means only one thing to anybody that studies this data: the dissatisfaction with our system is based on fallacious knowledge of the system. Thirty-three percent would be a rip-off. I think we all accept that. Seventeen percent would be a rip-off. But the dissatisfaction within our

---

"**Keep in mind that our system—we call it 'free enterprise'—has one priceless ingredient lacking in any other economic system. That ingredient is competition.... Competition keeps the action reasonable.**"

society rests and originates from this gross misconception.

Let's look at high-school student attitudes toward business. They are exactly what you would expect them to be. Are profits necessary for business health? No, said sixty-seven percent of the high-school students. Remember, economics is rarely taught in high schools. We insist that our young people have some knowledge of American history, be able to read, write, and speak the English language, have some knowledge of the sciences and the humanities. But we don't require them, in any sense, to have any comprehension of how our system works. That information doesn't get to them.

Should private industry or government provide all the jobs? Sixty-two percent said the government should provide all the jobs. That's socialism. Is socialism a better system than capitalism? The answer is just what you expected. Sixty percent of the students said yes. Should a worker produce all that he reasonably can? Sixty-one percent said no. What is the best way to increase our standard of living? Increase everybody's wages. Fifty-five percent of the people said that.

Now that has to be abysmal ignorance of our system. We lack philosophical compatibility because of this ignorance and misconception. I'm going to give you a figure here that staggers me, because at the college level economics *is* taught. A great percentage of university students do study economics, where the facts and figures and comparative ideologies are actually taught. So they should know the basic functioning of our system.

When this question, what is the average net after-tax profit to American corporations on their sales, was confined to college-level students, the consensus was no longer thirty-three percent. It was forty-five percent.

This is what a Gallup poll found. And if there is fact to this, one has to ask: what is being taught in our colleges and universities, and why? And I don't like to raise the question, but I think it should come to everyone's mind: Is the ignorance and misinformation simply neglect and omission, or is it contrived?

**Education in Free Enterprise System**

Getting down to the matter of priorities, the number-one

priority is to correct this misconception, to mandate in our school systems that our young people do get a firm grounding in how our system works, so that they will judge the system on the basis of what it is and not on the basis of what it isn't.

And I would be hopeful that as and when our society can judge our great system on the basis of what it is, that this would create the philosophical attitude that will permit a constructive and productive partnership between American business and government.

The government is here to stay. We all know that. The public sector is here. The private sector is not necessarily here to stay.

*The Moderator explains the "piggyback system": one speaker who has something relevant to add to what the last speaker just said can piggyback. Bob Strauss has asked to piggyback.*

**Robert Strauss**
*Ambassador*

I have seen those numbers and they are horrible. And it is true—it is due to a lack of knowledge on the part of the people of this country.

I agree that government is going to be here and we're not so sure about the other. The solution to the problem is the point I didn't get around to making. That is, we have a great failure in this country, a great unwillingness of people to get their hands dirty.

The reason there is so much misinformation is there are too few people who care enough—out of the business community, to begin with—to get involved. Bill Coors represents a point of view, and he represents it very strongly and very ably, and that point of view and other points of view ought to be heard.

---

**"The government is here to stay. We all know that. The public sector is here. But the private sector is not necessarily here to stay."**

93

What do we have to do in this country if we're ever going to get people involved? Businessmen and women, and people who are active in other sectors, are going to have to get involved and see their stories told. If business is going to survive and if government is going to get better, then they're going to have to get involved.

But the sad part about it is, you always see the same people at the same meetings. It's just like in charity. The same people give to build the church that give to the United Way, and the same people attend the same forums. You know who you are going to see, and you know who is going to be sitting on his can back home, or sitting in his office complaining about what's wrong with the country.

**John Swearingen**
*Chairman,*
Standard Oil of Indiana

*John Swearingen is the elected head of the American Petroleum Institute, and in that position is indeed the spokesman for the petroleum industry in this country. He is currently Chairman of Standard Oil of Indiana. Since he became Chief Executive of Standard Oil of Indiana the profits have grown from $145 million to a little over a billion dollars, a growth rate that is twice that in the petroleum industry at large. His company is leader in oil-well drilling in the United States, and is the sixth-largest United States oil company today. Mr. Swearingen also serves on the board of other companies and of two universities, Carnegie-Mellon and De Pauw.*

## Liberty and Responsibility

One thing we all have to keep in mind is that the revolutions of history have been caused by revolt of the people against oppressive government. We in this country, for the last two hundred years, have had a liberty which has been unusual in the life of the world. Those of us walking the streets and sitting in these chairs here today have never experienced the loss of liberty. I don't think most of us realize what the loss of liberty entails. We object, of course, when we find the government imposing restraints on our abilities to make choices of our own, whether it's as individuals or whether as businesses. We object to those things.

But I don't believe most of us really understand what the loss of liberty is. Liberty carries with it responsibility. Too few of us in this country assert ourselves to the extent necessary to make our views felt, not only in the setting of priorities in this country, but in the implementation of the priorities agreed upon.

There's a story going around about the three biggest lies in America. One is "I gave at the office," which Mr. Conway must know something about.

The second is "I'll call you back tomorrow."

And the third is "I'm from the Equal Employment Opportunity Commission and I'm here to help you."

I think anybody who has had any experience in running a business, or a university for that matter, may have some understanding of the wryness of this comment. Because government efforts to help frequently are a hindrance, or altogether nonproductive.

## Meaning of Partnership

One of the main things that has to be determined is what we mean by partnership. You can have a senior partner, you can have a junior partner, you can have a limited partner, you can have an equal partnership; but what's happening to us in this country is that the government is becoming more and more the senior partner in all the activities, personal, economic, and otherwise, in this country. It's assuming a life of its own. Until we redefine this partnership, I think we're going to continue to have some of the problems we have discussed so far.

I would like to see something like an equal partnership between the people in the business community and their elected representatives and the employees of the government. Obviously, the spectrum of how you can handle this runs all the way from the example of Russia, where the government determines behavior in everything, to a place, I suppose, like this country was a hundred years ago, where there were almost no restraints on individual activity. Somewhere in

---

"I would like to see something like an equal partnership between the people in the business community and their elected representatives and the employees of the government."

between might be an appropriate level. But I believe that the partnership has gotten out of whack.

We've raised the question whether the terms of service in the United States Congress were too long, whether some shouldn't be, by some manner or other, curtailed. There's a lot to support this point of view. Attempts to limit the longevity of people who are administering the government, to have a turnover, to have more citizen participation at every level, should be considered.

## Regulation

Those of us who run businesses experience problems with regulatory agencies every day. What we find is that the Congress has created many of these agencies that affect everything we do.

I suspect everyone in this room at some time or another has experienced a seat-belt problem. This is only the most obvious of the ways regulations affect our lives every day. We also find that the people who are making regulations are also the ones who administer them, and the ones who weigh and judge the results when complaints are made about the application of these regulations.

At least in general legal affairs, if there's a dispute among people you can go to the courts. You can argue your case. The judge will take into consideration past history in similar situations and arrive at a decision people can generally abide by.

In tax matters, there is a code of tax regulations that is continually revised. It now takes someone who spends his life to interpret them. But there is a tax court to which you can take your problems, independent of the people who drafted the regulations, and have a hearing for your case.

But there is no such thing with such regulatory agencies as the Environmental Protection Agency or the Occupa-

---

"We also find that the people who are making regulations are also the ones who administer them, and the ones who weigh and judge the results when complaints are made about the application of these regulations."

97

tional Safety and Health Administration, or many of these like the Equal Employment Opportunity Commission, the newer ones which have come into being in the last few years.

Mr. Strauss has just informed me that the Administration has taken the position that economic studies should be made of the impact of new regulations before they are put into place. This is one of the greatest things I've seen come out of this Administration. I'm delighted to see this done, because we're paying huge amounts of money for things we don't really want. If we are willing to sit down and look at the real cost of what we're doing, we'll come to better answers.

The question of the kind of partnership we want is important—do we want to have government responsive to the people, or do we want it the other way around? Once having settled that question and elected representatives to our legislative bodies to set priorities, then we should agree to try to support the priorities that have been set. We should not just say, "Look, we're going to riot in the streets; we're going to oppose these things because we don't agree. We're going to to try to delay, and by delay to kill, and use the law to our benefit to support our own special ends."

We've got to establish a basis for a partnership before we can establish priorities that we can agree on and pursue for a period of time for the benefit of all of us.

**Jack T. Conway**
*United Way of America*

### Consensus on Goals Needed

In the absence of any kind of coalition or consensus approach to goals, we have a tendency to approach everything in an adversary light. People who differ take their differences to the electoral process. Then when they count up who won and who lost they take it to the Congress. There's a constant process of trying to influence the outcome of the legislation in an adversarial context.

We went through a period of divided government when the President was of one party and the Congress was controlled by another party. In that kind of setup you get legislation initiated from the Congress without the benefit of the President's fine hand and recommendations and so on. So, first the differences tend to get exacerbated, and then finally the noses are counted, the votes are taken, and a law has been passed. Then the adversary process is shifted to influencing the race, and you simply carry this adversary process all the way through the system.

I think we've got to learn how to take the problem and structure it in such a way that we can build a consensus on how best to solve it. Then we should see if can build a consensus to take to the President and to the Congress on how to legislate to facilitate solving the problem. Such a consensus concerning the nature of the problem would make it unnecessary to have complex regulations to interpret what the law was intended to be or to do. Consensus would eliminate an awful lot of the trouble that we now seem to be experiencing around the country in almost everything we do.

We've turned out a whole generation of young lawyers. Lawyers are to litigate. Litigation is always in courts. So we end up being held up in courts on all kinds of things because some public-interest group was formed to push this particular point of view against another one which was formed to push another point of view. We never seem to agree on what it is we want to achieve in contrast to advancing our own particular interests.

A partnership, in my judgment, has to start off around some effort to set goals and achieve consensus and define the problem. Then I think the rest flows from that.

### John Swearingen
*Standard Oil Co. of Indiana*

One of the major issues dividing people in their attitudes toward specific questions is that of short-term versus long-term priorities. What do you want to do today for today and tomorrow and next week, as compared to what you want to have happen in a year or two years or ten years.

Too much of what was done in this country in the last ten or fifteen years has been based almost entirely on short-term emphasis in the priorities we set. What is right for the short term may be absolutely wrong for the long term.

99

Because we set short-term priorities of increasing our redistribution of wealth in this country in the last ten or fifteen years, we got behind in some of our long-term priorities. We're just now catching up to the fact that our military establishment has got a tremendous rebuilding problem ahead of it.

*The first question addressed to the panel on priorities for partnership, accusing American business with unconcern over the treatment of human rights by totalitarian governments, or the active support of such governments for economic reasons, stimulates the longest audience participation session of the entire conference.*

*Many important issues are examined, including negotiation and consensus among traditional adversaries, the habit of confrontation in this country, and the varied purposes of partnership, from increased productivity and more jobs to a more equitable society.*

*And yet, in effect, each speaker in the following discussion takes a course somewhat parallel but more or less unrelated to the other speakers. No common area of agreement, or even of disagreement, emerges in this discussion of priorities, as it did in the first discussion of the rationale behind partnership. We have here, in effect, an example of the difficulty in achieving agreement over priorities.*

### From the Audience:

I would like to address this to Mr. Coors. If the private business sector in the United States is so opposed to the suppression of human rights and so supportive of human freedom, then why does it so actively support, through trade, technology, and sometimes even covert means, totalitarian and oppressive governments in such places as South Africa, Iran, South Korea, and Uganda?

And what about the problem created by private industry in terms of the pollution that it has put into our air and into our streams? We are now having to face up to those problems. In many cases the government is having to clean up the mess that private industry has put on us in the areas of radioactive waste, Kepon asbestos, and others. Please address yourself to that.

**William K. Coors**
*Adolph Coors Company*

I think there are good reasons for what has happened ...

The private sector doesn't condone that kind of thing, and isn't in any conspiracy to support these governments. In many cases the political attitudes of both the private and public sectors in this country are determined by the desperate need for raw materials that come from these countries.

We all must be aware of the impact upon us of losing five percent of our oil supply. What do you do? Do you support a possibly tyrannical government in Iran in order to provide yourself with fuel? Or, do you *not* support that government and sacrifice that fuel, and intensify the energy problems here?

Those are the trade-offs that have been talked about. I believe what you addressed yourself to are really political expediencies with strong economic overtones. I don't think we're talking philosophies at all. I think we're talking the practicalities of the situation.

**Robert Strauss**
*Ambassador*

We just had a question in the government involving whether or not we were going to sell drill bits to Russia—a pretty good example of the dilemma you've been discussing.

We had two business concerns involved. They work together occasionally, and live within a few blocks of each other in Dallas, Texas. One wanted to sell drill bits and made quite an economic case for the fact that the drill bits should be sold. Drill bits represent, in a way, our technology.

The other company felt very strongly, philosophically, that it *shouldn't* be done. One company had an economic interest; I don't think the other did. But I don't think even with an economic interest that either company would have sacrificed the best interest of this nation. But they differed very strongly.

The philosophical as well as the economic issues were debated very heatedly. The government first ruled one way and then reopened it and ruled another way. I happen to think they ruled in the right way. The decision may have been good, it may have been bad. I'm no judge. But it represented the best of what ought to take place in the decisionmaking process in this country.

Government with responsibility, a strong private-sector involvement, a decision made by the governmental arm whose responsibility it was, and a rehearing and a change in decision. I think all parties felt rather good about the thing, even those who were on the losing side of the issue. We do a bit better job than the question would imply.

### William K. Coors
*Adolph Coors Company*

When we talk about some of the problems that industry finds itself with in terms of worker health, dangerous chemicals contaminating the environment, and so forth, it's very easy to blame industry for that.

But those who blame industry are always unaware of the fact that industry cannot police itself. There is no way the oil industry, or the alcoholic beverage industry, can get together and set up their own specific standards for what goes on, and police them. That is antitrust. You go to the penitentiary for that.

Here is where the partnership comes in. It is absolutely essential to our society that we do have a government that sets up these standards for us.

We don't object to the principle of uniform standards; we ask for realistic standards designed for adequacy rather than for the ultimate.

I point, for example, to the famous Muskie Pure Water Bill, passed in 1970 by a vote of 96 to 0 by the Senate. Overwhelming! Well, pure water is a sacred cow. It's become a sacred institution.

A number of years ago we had two sacred institutions in our country. One was motherhood and the other was the American flag. The environment, now, and the various aspects of the environment, are so sacred that it is not politically expedient to vote against them. If you study that so-called Water Bill, you will find that it comes up with the concept of zero return. Now zero return simply means that water, once it is taken out of any of the nation's water courses, cannot be returned unless that water is absolutely pure. This is not the way the bill is being administered today, but this is the objective of that bill.

When you think of the engineering challenge of returning water that pure to the nation's water courses, you realize that there is not the financial means to do it. In energy alone, it would more than double the energy requirements for our society. And it isn't necessary because we're not using water that is pure to begin with.

We endorse reasonable, consistent standards. But only to the degree that they are necessary for the health of our society.

**From the Audience:**

In reference to Jack Conway's statement, it appears to me that partnership implies mutual benefit. But I infer that a relatively small portion of our society today is based on that kind of partnership, and that the major portion is in the adversary relationship that Mr. Conway suggests.

I would guess that the members of the panel, and perhaps correctly so, would suggest that labor and management do better in an adversary relationship. Conceivably even labor's existence, or the unions' existence, may demand an adversary relationship, at least in the American society.

Further, I would suggest that lawyers tend to see the world in an adversary relationship such as Mr. Conway suggests. Since, in fact, this is so, and since they so substantially permeate our legislatures, how do you anticipate resolutions that come out in a partnership framework as opposed to an adversary framework?

**Robert Strauss**
*Ambassador*

I'm not so sure that we ever really defined "adversary" properly. I can't think of any tougher bargaining situations between labor and management than in the communication industry and the textile unions, where we still have these horrible strikes going on. Those are two with which I have considerable familiarity.

John DeButts, the most recent retiring chairman of AT&T, has said to me on a number of occasions that probably one of his strongest allies and supporters was Mr. Glenn Watts, the head of the Communication Workers Union. And here was a fellow with whom he had easily had his most serious and strenuous negotiating problems over the years. So, there they find themselves working together and working apart.

I've just finished trying to negotiate a textile arrangement, on behalf of the Administration, with one of the textile industries. Our aim was to strike a balance between inflation problems and consumer problems. Yet we had to keep the industry viable and keep employment up. This industry employs nearly three million people, sixty percent of them women or blacks or others who have trouble finding employment. It was essential we work that out.

The Labor-Management Committee worked together for a year, in harness. They worked exceedingly well together. When they left my office after four or five hours I'm sure they went right back into a terribly difficult negotiating posture.

I think it can be done. It depends on the kind of leadership and the kind of involvement you get. And it depends upon habits. Many aspects of confrontation in this country are habits. People get in the habit of being mean and nasty, or people get in the habit of being otherwise.

Robert Strauss    *Discussion*
Ambassador

I believe in the people of this country, in the sectors of this country, and in the resources of this country. I feel strongly about our failure to tap them properly. And when I say "our" failure, I mean it's a governmental failure; it's a business failure; it's a failure of a great many of us. The kind of people who care enough to come to this conference are the ones who bear a very heavy responsibility, in my judgment.

I hope we'll discharge it, because as I said, the 1980s are an entirely different world. A much lower growth in that pie to be cut up. That's when it gets tough: when there isn't as much to divide around.

### John Swearingen
*Standard Oil Co. of Indiana*

May I just add, during World War II the priorities of the nation were well established and accepted by everyone. The business-government partnership was what enabled us to win the war, by producing the materials and getting them to the place we needed them when we needed them. It can be done again.

### Jack T. Conway
*United Way of America*

In the twenty-four years that I was with the Auto Workers Union, I was an advocate of the adversary relationships. It was necessary during that period of time. We had to establish an equilibrium and a set of procedures for resolving problems.

It took a long time to do. Eventually, you couldn't find a more sophisticated, civilized group of people on both sides of the bargaining table than you find now in the auto industry and the Auto Workers Union. They have the capacity to fight furiously over detail and also to fashion an agreement that they can live with. They can also address problems in their communities when they put aside their adversarial relationship and approach things on a community basis. There's been an evolution in that sense.

My two years in the public-employee sector shook me and some of my attitudes because the relationships there are not limited to the employer and the employees. There are many other parties to the bargaining process: the taxpayers, the citizens of the community, the people who receive the services and the people who deliver them.

In the public-employee context, bringing these different interests into the process so that their needs are considered is critical. That's exactly what finally happened in New York City. The employees of the City could not decide whether or not to charge tuition in the City University. If tuition were not charged, the employees of the university were going to lose jobs. It was going to be necessary to shut down the university, or to amalgamate it into the State University system.

There were all kinds of different interests. Should the employee pension funds be used to buy the MAC bonds that would keep the city going? We couldn't make that decision by ourselves. There was a law that precluded it on books. We had to go to Albany and get an agreement.

Everybody had to go up—the bankers, the unions, the city officials—and address the legislature on a common program to change the law to permit the unions to buy the bonds that would keep the city from going bankrupt. That practice of defining the problem, structuring it, figuring out what needed to be done, and then addressing the problem, difficult as it may be, was the experience that Felix was talking about earlier. The kinds of problems we face as a nation are going to require that same kind of approach, in my judgment, and we haven't had much practice at it. I think we ought to start. The sooner we start, the sooner we'll be able to do something about these problems.

**From the Audience:**

Mr. Conway is the only one who's really given any example of where partnership works. Mr. Coors said we're living in a time of misconception and misinformation. Mr. Swearingen said that the employers and government won World War II with production. Bob Strauss said that we've got to have a partnership of government and business and others, and I suppose "others" would cover a lot of people. What do Mr. Coors and Mr. Swearingen think concerning labor's role in a partnership involved in solving these problems?

**John Swearingen**
*Standard Oil Co. of Indiana*

Well, obviously, labor is a part of this. Business has no desire to force people to do work they don't want to do. Business could set some policies, but if the labor isn't available to carry those through, the job won't be done. I was talking about business as a whole, including both management and labor, in the context of my remarks.

**William K. Coors**
*Adolph Coors Company*

Based on my own empirical experience and no more, dealing with unions that have representative employees in my company: I have never found anything but an adversary relationship.

What has always worried me the most about this relationship is my conviction that much of this misconception and misinformation that I spoke about earlier has been coming to our people from their unions. There is a constant barrage of antimanagement sentiment—propaganda, if you will. It goes on twenty-four hours a day, 365 days of the year.

And it's very easy to do because management is people. People make mistakes. Management can bat 999, but the 999 successes are ignored and the one error is blown up out of the water.

Now, if labor and management are going to be partners, what first has to be developed is a philosophical compatibility. I have yet—and I've done a lot of negotiating—to talk to a labor leader who didn't ask for more money for less work. Remember, my experience is not as broad as is the experience of the other gentlemen here.

But I have never seen a labor leader yet who was willing and anxious to say, "Look, give us ten percent more and we'll work with you to get ten percent greater productivity."

Productivity is the name of the game. The productivity of any society is directly proportional to the standard of living of that society. The basic reason we are suffering from inflation and our standard of living is going down is that our productivity is going down for all kinds of reasons.

If we're going to have a three-way partnership—government, labor, and business—the basic purpose of that partnership should be to increase productivity, which increases purchasing power. It's not the dollars in the paycheck that should be of concern. It's what those dollars can buy.

**Jack T. Conway**
*United Way of America*

The labor movement is not monolithic, any more than the business community is monolithic. Different industries have different problems and different unions.

I cite my own experience in the auto industry. In 1948, we wrote right into contracts, and it's there to this day, that we are in favor of the best machinery and equipment. Our wages are determined on a formula basis to protect against the cost of living, and also to reflect increases in productivity. Written right into the agreement. Believe in it.

As I say, that industry, which represents a massive part of American industry, has rationalized its relationships. It no longer feuds over these kinds of things. That doesn't mean that they are married to each other, inseparable in the broadest sense. They've accommodated, and it's the accommodation that permits other kinds of relationships in working together.

The question of what's a fair day's work for a fair day's pay is the most debated thing in the world. It depends on whether you're doing it or you're paying for it. And it will happen every time. There's no way to get away from it.

You'll never settle the philosophical question before you proceed to the next set of problems. So just let that one lay.

**From the Audience:**

What are we doing to produce more jobs? This is a concern to the university students. Are we so computerized, mechanized, that nobody is creating any more jobs? How many jobs are we going to need in this country? Is business doing anything to create more jobs? They're going to have to pick up more of the tab if we are to reduce the federal payroll.

**Robert Strauss**
*Ambassador*

We're setting records almost every month. In November of last year [1978], we created more jobs than have ever been created in one month in the history of the nation, in the private sector. We've been creating close to half a million jobs a month, for many months, in this country. Never have there been as many jobs created, never have there been as many people working, over a single period of time, as there were during the year 1978.

How many jobs—that's a good question. A good deal is going on that's very positive. Now, as we retool, as we need to do, as we modernize, as we computerize, it's going to be a difficult job, a different problem again.

We need to slow this thing down if we're going to get ahead, and get hold of inflation. As the GNP slows a bit during the year 1979, that slowdown is going to produce a dip, and then a rise again in unemployment. Six months from now, I suspect, we're going to be talking again about unemployment.

You get back into that question of how much pain do you inflict on one group? How much can you inflict to accommodate the national good, which is to get our hands on the inflation that's destroying so many of us here? Those are the kinds of trade-offs we're talking about.

These are very wrenching questions; they're not easy to answer. You can go into a meeting certain you are going to come down on one side, and end up on an altogether different side.

### Jack T. Conway
*United Way of America*

We still have the serious structural unemployment problem in the inner cities and among minority groups that seems to defy all efforts to help. We have to bring that whole set of problems back up on the front burner again and make another strenuous effort to do something about it.

That touches on what I think is one of the most serious problems facing this nation. We are developing in this country a subculture of people who never have had a job, have given up looking for a job, don't even know how to look for a job. Primarily the young inner-city black. This nation is paying a price for this situation, one that is foreign and alien to us.

We haven't touched that subject. It's a hard core out there that is—I call it a subculture—that is a rather sinister sort of thing, but it's true. It's alien to America. We can't seem to get in and crack that. As well as we're going in every other area, we're just beginning to make some inroads there. The government can't seem to solve it. Hell, they have tried and fallen on their faces a number of times.

This kind of problem, hard-core unemployables, is where you need to get your hands on the John Swearingens of this country and really put them to work. Now, Peter McCullough and a group at Xerox did some work on that. Bill Miller, now chairman of the Fed, worked on it. A number of other people have; but we just don't have the answer to it.

### John Swearingen
*Standard Oil Co. of Indiana*

There is a lot of misinformation about this subject. I don't for one minute want to say that black teenagers who don't have a job are *not* a problem for themselves and a problem for society. They are. But the figures batted about are that some thirty to thirty-five percent of these black teenagers are without jobs, and they are in pockets in the disadvantaged areas of the cities.

I think the statistics are misleading, because these black teenagers—just think about it—teenagers, meaning 16 to 19 year-olds—are high school dropouts. When you look at the population available for work, most of those 16 to 19 year-olds are still in school.

Consider the entire population of people, not just the ones looking for jobs; the unemployment among black teenagers is more like ten to twelve percent instead of the thirty to thirty-five percent that is batted about as being the horrible problem.

It is a problem, but it is not a problem that is going to be cured by balancing the federal budget or controlling interest rates or doing other things on a macroeconomic scale in order to try to fight inflation. The government has been wrong in trying to cure this kind of problem with macroeconomic tools.

As far as private industry is concerned, it has done a great deal in trying to provide jobs in these areas. We have done a considerable amount of this on our own by fostering and establishing businesses in disadvantaged areas. One of the biggest contributions we have made is to provide markets for products that can be turned out by black-owned businesses.

I think this has been one of the great success stories of American business. I'm happy to say our own company has been in the lead in this. There is no point in manufacturing a product if you can't sell it. But American industry has been able to do something to alleviate employment problems. We have accomplished some wonderful things in that regard.

**Robert Strauss**
*Ambassador*

I want to disagree with you some there. This is more than 16 to 19 year-olds. It involves people who are 22 and 24. It's a broader problem than just teenagers. Many of these young people are unemployable. I understand that. The trick is not getting them into something where you manufacture products that can't be sold. Of course it's a difficult problem. Business and government have been working together on it and trying hard. And both have failed, in my judgment, despite their good efforts. The trick is, how do you get these people integrated into the business community where they are manufacturing and working at producing something that can be sold profitably? So they can earn and get off welfare, pay taxes, and be productive members of this society?

I don't have the answer. This government doesn't have the answer. Private industry doesn't have it, and labor doesn't have it. We have all been working on it. I'm faulting us for lack of performance; I'm faulting us for some lack of attention—not for our lack of concern.

Just because we defined a problem we haven't solved doesn't mean we have to find fault. I don't bring up the fault in people. I thing we've all done a lot, but a lot more needs to be done. Too often in this country, when there is an unsolved problem, we ask who in the hell we are going to blame it on?

We don't always have to blame something on somebody. It's something we have to cure. It's almost like a disease you get. You don't blame it on the one you caught it from. You've got to cure the darn thing and the quicker the better, because it is debilitating. This is a very debilitating thing in our society.

### From the Audience:

Bob Strauss mentioned something a moment ago I also am concerned with: inflation and the public debt. The deficit the government is creating, in my mind, is creating additional inflation. I don't see any improvement in either inflation or in our public debt, except it's going up and we have to pay more interest every year. I am concerned. Can anybody give me an answer?

### Robert Strauss
*Ambassador*

The question you raised is the most serious question on the minds of the American people today. I, too, am concerned about our deficit, and I think all of America is concerned, including the President.

I would point out that in 1976, our deficit was around 65, 66 billion dollars. I hope we'll make a 30 billion dollar deficit this year; we're going in the right direction. Now, 30 billion dollars is way too big a deficit, but it is a hell of a lot better than 65 or 66. It's awfully hard to get the darn thing down any faster than that. I've been involved in the budget-cutting processes. You know I'm rather a fiscal conservative.

You talked about the foreign countries. Here's a very little known fact: We look at West Germany and think of it as the classic economic model we ought to follow. A great many people do that. Many economists and businessmen keep referring to it. It *is* good.

The annual deficit in West Germany, as a percentage of its gross national product, is higher than in this country. The same with Japan.

I didn't know that until about eight months ago. I'm sure glad somebody gave me a chance to show how smart I am, because it's a rather interesting statistic. I'm not sure I know what it means, but it sounds good. And interestingly enough, West Germany will probably have a three-percent inflation rate this year with that.

It's an amazing thing. A three-percent inflation, a deficit that's a higher percentage of GNP than our own. I don't know how they do it. How do you get to deficit financing?

Do you have a constitutional amendment or a convention or what do you do?

West Germany, for example, unless they pass a constitutional amendment, or some kind of exception, they cannot run a deficit. Every year they find the exception and they just keep going on.

I don't know what the answer is to these problems. They do affect inflation. We are trying to come to grips with them, with some success. Not enough to satisfy me, not enough to satisfy the President, and not enough to show up. My judgment is, by summer, you are going to see some help; not before.

**From the Audience:**

Mr. Conway, what kind of philosophy or goals will

motivate us to accomplish the trade-offs you suggest? Is productivity a long-term goal on a planet of limited resources?

**Jack T. Conway**
*United Way of America*

We don't have commonly accepted goals right now, and we need them. I would suggest that we start around these four intractable areas by developing an effective energy policy, recognizing that it is going to be a higher cost energy policy that is going to contribute to inflationary pressures. But it will produce the revenues that will lead to the exploration and development of energy sources so that we can become less dependent on the outside world. That's one set of problems.

It seems to me we have to talk that thing through in public so everybody understands it. When Schlesinger says that the cost of gasoline is going to be $1.00 per gallon next year the people ought to understand why, and what the effects of that are. And then, having in a sense given a rational set of objectives, you have to move to the inflation thing, taking into consideration what you've just done in the energy side, and begin to address the question of how you bring inflation under control.

Everything is indexed now. Everybody calculates their business decisions for the next three or four years based upon an inflation rate. It's built right into every calculation we make. We have wages adjusted to it, taxes that reflect it.

We've got to do certain things which will affect people; the trade-offs of lower inflation compared with giving up some things, for example, have to be clearly understood by everybody. That, then, becomes an objective that can be incorporated in the kind of an agreed-upon set of goals.

Again in the trade area, as Bob Strauss has said, we have tough problems. If you modernize the steel industry so that you can compete with Japanese and Korean and German steel, you are going to have more Youngstowns, because you are going to have modern steel mills instead of obsolete steel mills. And the chances are, they are going to be located in communities other than the ones that are currently steel towns.

Those are top social problems we have to face. Now, how do you deal with that? The ramifications of trade policy are a community problem as well as a national problem. It's terribly important that we compete and that we bring our trade deficits down. It's terribly important that we deal as a most favored nation with as many nations as we can, and keep as open a trade policy as we can. The trade thing has an effect on employment, because people are dislocated. We've got to take these things into consideration and develop some adjustment programs. How do you move people from one kind of industry to another, one kind of job to another, perhaps even one community to another, as you get shutdowns or adjustments that are larger than the community can adjust to?

But these are long-term things. They are not tomorrow's problems. I think John Swearingen is absolutely right. Too frequently we get confused and pass a law to deal with today's problem tomorrow, when in fact what we do today to deal with tomorrow's problems creates the problem that we have to deal with next year.

We're not thinking ahead far enough, and we're not integrating our objectives. The trade-offs become clear when you do that. That's not business's business or government's business or labor's business; it's all of our business. What we do affects all of us.

**From the Audience:**

How, specifically, do you propose to separate these tasks of government regulation and administrative agencies among the private and public sectors, and maintain the integrity of the reason for regulation?

**John Swearingen**
*Standard Oil Co. of Indiana*

You are asking a very difficult question here. I personally think some kind of a court or legal system is needed in each of these major agencies to deal with interpretation of regulation. There is no such thing now. This is not going to come into being overnight, but I think it's the only fair way to do it.

An attempt should be made to determine whether regulations have outlived their purposes. A number of Sunset Bills are now under consideration in the Congress, and there is a great debate as to whether this should continue or not.

Some of these regulations have outlived their usefulness, and ought to be abandoned altogether. But this is an evolutionary process; there is not going to be any major change overnight. I'm just delighted that the Administration is going to attempt to make an economic-impact evaluation of regulations before they are put into effect. This doesn't say anything about those that are already in place; I hope that will be the next step. If we are going to continue this regulatory process we've got to have an appeal system, which we don't have now.

**From the Audience:**

I was not very well satisfied with the answer to a very important part of an earlier question, that as we become more computerized and more competitively tooled, we're going to have a more difficult time providing jobs.

Recent history has shown that the more competitively tooled we are, vis-a-vis the folks on the other side of the water, the more we're involved with the some temporary displacements with severe social consequences. But generally speaking, the better tooled we are the more competitive we are going to be internationally, and the more jobs we'll ultimately create for these folks coming up who need them. I think this issue might provide a reason for partnership that nobody has really gotten a handle to. Why do we need to get together?

**Robert Strauss**
*Ambassador*

My daily responsibility is to run a balanced trade

116

program for this nation. I have tremendous support from the President; he takes a lot of political heat for running an enlightened and progressive trade program, I don't say that in a partisan way because the Republican leadership in the Congress has been equally supportive.

Let me show you the kind of problems we deal with. First, you talk about a tool-up. Business is not really bad in the textile industry, and we are turning out a lot more products right now. But there's been a lot of dislocation and unemployment in the textile industry. We've had some loss of jobs even though we've had an expansion of the industry due to modernization.

I'm in favor of that modernization, because it serves the nation well. But it does create short-run and even long-run dislocations. We deal with that kind of problem in every industry.

The shoe industry is a good example. We are not modernized there, and where we're not modernized we're not competitive. Where we are competitive there is a considerable job loss. We're torn on the one hand between protecting those jobs that you are concerned about, and correctly so, and we're concerned on the other hand about how much support to give the shoe industry by keeping out foreign shoes and having the customer pay a higher price for shoes.

Then, you go on to the sugar industry. We have a price support in sugar, to keep sugar farmers working so we don't have terrible unemployment and displacement everywhere from Idaho to Louisiana and Texas. That means that the American sugar consumer has to pay a bit more for sugar. You say it's just a couple of dollars more a year, but it adds a little maybe to candy and to soft drinks and to other things. It runs up.

You have to preserve the industry; you have to save the jobs; you have to balance that against the consumer interest, and it's tough.

Let's bring it close to home now. The governors and the mayors want revenue-sharing; revenue-sharing means spending money. The cities want tax-free municipals, and they ought to have them. They have to finance their affairs.

Without tax-free municipals they wouldn't be able to raise the money to do certain things they ought to be doing.

Consider the steel industry. We're trying to avoid the terrible tragedy of these cities where the steel mills have had to fold. In order to do that, what do you have to do? You raise the price of steel a little. I'm not objecting to raising the price of steel a little to keep the plants open and keep the people working. Nor do I object to the argument on the other hand: let it all come in and get steel in here a little cheaper.

These are not simple answers. You're never right. It's a balancing constantly of how you do it. A slide rule won't help you a darned bit. I found that out. You just have to kind of guess by your belly what is going to be best, and hope you are right. Sometimes you are.

That isn't a very encouraging thing to say, but in every single industry we have that. Look at the computer industry and the aircraft industry. What do you do to keep our very dominant position there? Do you try to keep out foreign suppliers or do you let them become competitive? Where do you strike the balance?

What I'm trying to show you is that we don't have the answers because the answers aren't pat. You are looking at the fellow who was the world's greatest expert on how you ought to raise children, because there were three of the worst little old kids I ever saw that lived next door to us, before *we* had a child.

But, a strange thing happened to me. The more children we had, the less of an expert I became. I didn't know: how late can they stay out, who can they go out with, should they start smoking, can they start driving, do they need shoes, how much should their allowance be? I never could answer a one of those questions, and they had seemed so simple. Yet I just had to do it.

# IV Overcoming Fundamental Barriers to Partnership

Introduction: **Donald Rice,**
RAND Institute

Moderator: **Peter Flawn,**
President and
Leonidas T. Barrow Professor,
The University of Texas at Austin

Panelists: **Harvey Kapnick,**
Chairman,
Arthur Andersen & Co.

**Ira Millstein,**
Partner,
Weil, Gotshal and Manges

**Joseph Swidler,**
Partner,
Leva, Hawes, Symington,
Martin and Oppenheimer

# Summary: Barriers to Partnership

We may not have sharply and crisply defined all the existing barriers inhibiting or preventing a partnership or even simply a better working relationship between business and government. We have identified, however, two major barriers to harmonious relations between the two giant sectors of American society: federal regulations and inadequate or spurious cost-accounting.

The regulatory system is simply not working, and nobody has the "plumbing" to deal with it. Although no quick solutions to administrative reform seem in sight, it is agreed that there is a real need for reform. One major criticism is that the regulatory agencies are not coordinated in their activities; another is that alternative ways of achieving the same social goals, more attractive to business, are not fairly considered. Yet another is that the federal agencies haven't benefited from the sunlight of full disclosure or from sunset laws closing up the doors of agencies which have outlived their usefulness.

Although it is agreed that the regulatory problem is enormously complex, and that there are one hundred possible approaches, some suggestions are made to begin reform: Congress might ask the President to check up on the agencies, since no one person has this responsibility; regulatory impact statements, including the costs of implementing regulations and the burdens to consumers, might be made mandatory.

Concerning costs and disclosure, it can be argued that a significant contributing cause to New York City's financial troubles was decentralized cost accounting. No one person knew just how deeply New York City was getting into trouble until the point of desperation was reached. Is the whole of the United States falling to problems of inadequate cost accounting? Mr. Kapnick points out that the United States is publishing only cash balances and not total legal obligations. Again we see the theme, noted earlier, that the habitual tools of business might suit the needs of the government—or rather, the needs of the people government represents and to whom it is accountable.

Whether business and government should indeed foster partnership is again debated. It is quickly agreed that a better working relationship is essential to achieve common national goals.

The emergence of single-issue voting groups and the mixed effects of the recent rise of participatory democracy are examined in relation to the indentification of common goals. Someone is needed to speak for the center, and trade-offs will be required to achieve the overall public interest. But the fact that none can agree what the overall public interest *is* is also brought up.

We are looking for a way of balancing the public and the private good. It is mentioned, however, that while economic strength has in the past been assumed as a base from which to launch solutions to other pressing national problems, now maintaining economic strength in the face of international competition is a priority in itself.

Business and government are made up of people; the unwillingness to take risks, like the hesitation to get involved, is mentioned as a deplorable contemporary attitude.

# IV Overcoming Fundamental Barriers to Partnership

**Donald Rice**
*President,*
RAND Institute

*From 1965 to 1967 Donald Rice was a professor at the Naval Graduate Institute and the University of California. In 1967 he became Director of Cost Analysis in the Office of the Secretary of Defense; two years later he was appointed Deputy Assistant Secretary for Resource Analysis. Between 1970 and 1972 he served as Assistant Director of the Office of Management and Budget in the Executive Office. Since 1972 he has been President of the RAND Institute, a nonprofit public-service institution devoted to research and to national security and domestic affairs issues.*

## New Institutions for Social and Economic Regulation

I was asked to talk about overcoming fundamental barriers to partnership between business and government. The very fact that this symposium is being held, and has attracted the kind of people who are here, attests to at least two realities. One is that the extent of government-business relationships has grown dramatically; and two, that the state of these relations is confused, if not chaotic, from some people's point of view.

The interests of government and business are bound together, at least at government initiative, by regulatory policy; by tax policy and fiscal policy; by the tariffs and quotas and international agreements of foreign trade; by the stockpiling of critical materials; by government procurement used to promote social and economic objectives; by government credit programs and insurance and subsidies; and so on and so on.

For example, the National Commission on Supplies and Shortages, a group that George Kozmetsky and I served on together some years ago, in responding to the national concern over shortages of materials that showed up in the early '70s, observed that: "Government policies influence when and where mines will be developed; they influence the technologies that will be used to extract ore and process it into finished material; they influence the price that this finished material can be sold for; they influence the ways in which this material will be used; and, when it reaches the end of its useful life, whether it will be discarded or recycled. Government policies and programs affect every stage of the material cycle. Sometimes the government is aware of this influence; more often it is not." [1]

To put it another way, this conference has cast an awfully wide net. As I said, I'd like to narrow it down some by focusing on the great growth area in government-business relationships, namely, regulatory policy, particularly the new regulation.

### Objectives of Cooperation

Before doing that, it seems worthwhile to stipulate that cooperation is not an end in itself. Cooperation is worth

---

"The interests of government and business are bound together, at least at government initiative, by regulatory policy; by tax policy and fiscal policy; by the tariffs and quotas and international agreements of foreign trade; by stock-piling of critical materials; by government procurement used to promote social and economic objectives; by government credit programs and insurance and subsidies; and so on and on."

pursuing to the extent it helps increase the size and quality of the pie to be divided among all the members of our society. Business activities can also contribute to social ends many people in our country consider essential to the quality of life.

The main issue I would like to raise for your consideration is whether our institutions are capable of meeting the burdens the government, generally with broad public support, has imposed upon them over the last decade or so. I will suggest that the answer is no, and that major changes are indicated on both sides of the relationship, but particularly on the government side.

**Regulation**

The most visible sign of the problem I would like to discuss is the tremendous increase in social and economic regulation and, most particularly, the proliferation of issue-specific regulatory bodies that have involved the government in virtually every aspect of business decisionmaking. Without asking whether these bodies are suited to this task, or investigating the broader implications of what it was doing, the government has applied an institutional form (proved relatively successful when applied elsewhere in our economy) to a totally new range of activities.

By requiring that the government clean up the environment, protect consumers from unsafe products, protect workers from hazardous work-place conditions, and eliminate discrimination through quasi-independent semijudicial agencies of government, we have created the basis for government-business conflict. While such conflict is not necessarily inappropriate, there are signs that it has become destructive.

The issue is not whether some degree of government-business cooperation is desirable; of course it is. The issue is whether the proper degree of such cooperation is achievable, given the institutions we have created and the task we have set for those institutions.

In a recent paper on economic policy, John T. Dunlop describes the "unparalleled expansion in the scope and detail of government penetration into private decisions."[2] He calls for a reduction in our use of legal institutions and an increased use of negotiation and compromise.

Charlie Schultze, the current chairman of President Carter's Council of Economic Advisors, in his widely admired Godkin Lectures, pointed out the perils of command and control regulation. Schultze called for the increased use of market incentives to achieve our regulatory goals—a plea similar to Dunlop's for decreased reliance on legal institutions.

Philip Abelson, the publisher of *Science* magazine, with his continued call in *Science* for the interjection of more scientific judgment into regulatory decisionmaking, has a similar objective in mind.

All these suggestions could improve the results of the current process. Yet they all stop short of dealing with the problem of the institutional structure that regulation virtually dictates.

Within such an institutional framework, reduced conflict between one set of actors—for example, government and business—usually means excluding others from the dialogue. In regulatory affairs, if government were to rely more on business advisory committees, or were to pay closer attention to the problems that business faces in dealing with regulation, there would arise a strong, and perhaps not unjustified, suspicion that this new relationship with business would result in less attention to what is perceived as the public interest.

### Conflict and Chaos

Our current regulatory institutions encourage conflict between the government and business, between business and public interest groups, and even between governmental institutions. The implicit theory seems to be that from this

---

"The issue is not whether some degree of government-business cooperation is desirable; of course it is. The issue is whether the proper degree of such cooperation is achievable, given the institutions we have created and the task we have set for those institutions."

conflict the true public interest will emerge. However, once we find government involving itself in the level of detail it currently engages in, the possibility of achieving the public interest is not all that certain.

At the same time, this enlarged government involvement with previously private decisions is carried out by several different agencies of government in a largely uncoordinated way. The National Commission on Supplies and Shortages that I referred to earlier, plus John Dunlop, plus George Eads, who is about to become a member of President Carter's Council of Economic Advisors, plus numerous other commentators, have noted that the left hand of government doesn't know what the right hand is doing. Furthermore, this governmental chaos, observers agree, visits several problems on private decisionmakers. The most obvious of these problems are much greater uncertainty, a short-term perspective, and the forced inefficient use of resources.

As George Eads has put it: "It often is the case that one regulatory body will be totally unaware that another body is contemplating (or, indeed, has already taken) an action that impacts crucially upon an action that the first agency is considering. In such cases, the business firm finds itself in the somewhat awkward position of explaining to the government what the government itself is doing."[3]

To acquire a better understanding of the alternatives available to us for doing a better job and to understand the trade-offs, the costs, and the consequences, will be a major undertaking. For example, some of these same observers I've been citing have noted that even if we could coordinate the

---

"Our current regulatory institutions encourage conflict between the government and business, between business and public interest groups, and even between governmental institutions. The implicit theory seems to be that from this conflict the true public interest will emerge. However, once we find government involving itself in the level of detail it currently engages in, the possibility of achieving the public interest is not all that certain."

efforts of the separate regulatory agencies, it is not at all clear we would know how to do it. We need much more analysis, by sector and by industry, of the combined effects of government regulations and other policies in order to understand the costs and benefits, including who pays the costs and who gets the benefits. Continued emphasis on aggregate economic analysis is simply insufficient as a guide to policy.

### Modifying Our Institutions

What, then, is the answer to all this? Well, there are at least two alternatives. One, which business might applaud, but which the public is not likely to accept, is to scale back the level of government involvement in the affairs of business to a level that our institutions are capable of coping with. Certain goals that Congress has mandated would be abandoned. We would give up our quest for a clean environment, safe consumer products, and a safe work place. Such a move would certainly reduce the level of government-business conflict. But it almost as certainly would raise the level of conflict elsewhere in our society, perhaps to intolerable levels. As I guess you can tell, I am not suggesting we take that alternative seriously, though some do.

The second alternative is to undertake the extremely complex and long-term job of modifying our institutions to make them more capable of handling the tasks assigned to them. I say "more capable" because I'm not sure that some of our goals can be achieved, regardless of our institutional arrangements.

Now, what might this alternative entail? The first step, it seems to me, would be recognizing that the many regulatory goals are sometimes mutually conflicting and, in any event, cannot all be achieved at once. John Dunlop put it well:

---

**"We need much more analysis, by sector and by industry, of the combined effects of government regulations and other policies in order to understand the costs and the benefits, including who pays the costs and who gets the benefits."**

". . . in mature relations no one confuses demands with reality to the extent politicians do in the economic arena."[4] That insight reminds me of Baldy's Law, an old engineering maxim that says, "Some of it plus the rest of it equals all of it."

## Trade-Offs and Objectives

Once we recognize that our resources are limited and that trade-offs have to be made among equally laudable objectives, we have a start on a solution. Today, many of our regulatory institutions are more answerable to the Congressional committees that created or oversee them than they are to the Executive, even though regulatory agency activities impinge on policy trade-offs properly made at the highest executive level.

We need to develop a clear understanding that the President or his staff have the authority to make such trade-offs among national goals, deciding which will be achieved and at what priority. That's the major institutional change required. For example, with regard to an industry like steel or autos, it should be quite clear that the President has the power to decide whether pollution reduction, energy efficiency, price stability, product quality, regional economic development, or international trade goals will be paramount and, given this decision, how regulatory and other policies ought to be harmonized.

Such executive authority would require legislation. Congress's role would be to identify the goals that ought to be given weight and to monitor the President's implementation of these objectives to guard against abuses of Executive discretion. But achieving any one social goal would not, as it is now, be legislatively declared paramount and immutable. Baldy's Law would again be recognized along the banks of the Potomac.

---

"Once we recognize that our resources are limited and that trade-offs have to be made among equally laudable objectives, we have a start on a solution."

Some would call the resultant process "national economic planning." I wouldn't, but I don't necessarily object to the term, used in that limited context. What is going on today is surely a major, usually inadvertent, level of national economic planning. If the Congress were asked to vote such major economic planning at the national level up or down all at once, it would surely be voted down.

## Adapting to Status Quo

What if we don't make our regulatory structure more rational, along the lines I have suggested? My view of the future, in that event, is somewhat different than you might expect. The current level of government-business conflict is unsustainable. Without changes of the sort I have been suggesting, business will adapt, and will begin to find out how to use the current set of institutions to its own ends.

Roger Noll, an economist at Cal Tech, has summarized the lessons we should learn from the more traditional economic regulation of industry. He graphically categorizes the social costs of the regulatory process as (1) "Penncentralization" (that's impairing incentives to operate efficiently); (2) "Lockheedization" (that's subsidizing inefficient firms); (3) "Legislation" (that's requiring endless red tape); and (4) "Consultation" (that's diverting scarce talent from the production to the redistribution of wealth). Noll also notes that empirical studies of the regulatory process and its results show that, over time, the regulated firms learn how to capture the process and turn it to their own ends, and the regulatory agencies become rigid and myopic, retarding innovation and competition wherever they threaten the existing institutional structure.[5]

Thus, what we should expect of business if the new regulation continues unabated is that, rather than compete in the market place, firms will find it much more comfortable to try to influence the government to use the regulatory process in ways that will disadvantage their competitors. Innovations will come to be judged not by the criterion of "Will it sell?" but against the criterion, "Can we induce the government to adjust its regulations so as to guarantee a market?"

Donald Rice
RAND Institute

Indeed, already there are signs that business is beginning to find the current regulatory environment, as chaotic and conflict ridden as it is, much to its liking. In the case of some current RAND research to examine the possibility of implementing market-oriented regulatory solutions, some of the strongest opposition we have encountered has come from business. Faced with the choice of a tax or marketable permit that would treat all equally situated polluters equally, business—at least many people in business—would opt for the current command and control system, believing, not without justification, that this system can be turned to advantage.

What of the business side of the relationship? What changes are needed there? It seems to me that business could do several things to help.

First, it could avoid the double standard of being against regulation except when it benefits.

Second, it could push, and push hard, for coordinated policies on the part of the government.

Third, it could make clear that it shares great social goals and is being innovative about how to accomplish them.

Fourth, it could devote some resources to increasing the knowledge base of the process. For example, Michael Novak, in an essay on the future of democratic capitalism,[6] has suggested that major corporations should support small, scholarly, in-house groups that do theoretical and empirical analyses of the corporation's involvement with public policies, and should also support a few independent public policy research groups working in fields of mutual business-government interest.

None of these ideas provide a panacea for all that ails the business-government relationship in the United States. Yet it seems clear to me that the new regulation, particularly in its

---

"What we should expect of business if the new regulation continues unabated is that . . . innovations will come to be judged not by the criterion of 'Will it sell?' but against the criterion, 'Can we induce the government to adjust its regulations so as to guarantee a market?'"

current institutional form, makes cooperative relationships that might serve the public interest much more difficult. Modifying our regulatory institutions in some fundamental ways, ways intended to expand the Executive's ability to identify and make trade-offs between conflicting goals, combined perhaps with a modest scaling back of our regulatory goals, will reduce some of the present level of government-business conflict. Such modifications of our regulatory institutions need not reduce the creative tension that should exist between the various segments of our economy.

## References

[1] *Government and the Nation's Resources: A Report of the National Commission on Supplies and Shortages* (Washington, D.C.: Government Printing Office, December 1976).

[2] "New Approaches to Economic Policy," *Regulation*, January-February 1979, pp. 13-14.

[3] "Chemicals as a Regulated Industry," Rand Corporation # P-6198 (February 1979), p. 14.

[4] "New Approaches to Economic Policy," *Regulation*, January-February 1979, p. 13.

[5] "The Social Costs of Governmental Intervention," in *The Business-Government Relationship,* ed. Neil H. Jacoby (Salt Lake City: Goodyear Publishing Co., 1978), pp. 56-64.

[6] *The American Vision* (Washington, D.C.: American Enterprise Institute, 1978).

**Peter Flawn**
*President and
Leonidas T. Barrow Professor,*
The University of Texas
at Austin

*Dr. Peter Flawn, an internationally known geologist, became President of The University of Texas at Austin in September 1979. He joined The University of Texas Bureau of Economic Geology in 1949, and now holds an endowed professorship in the Department of Geological Sciences and a position in the Lyndon B. Johnson School of Public Affairs. He has held high administrative posts at The University of Texas at Austin, including Executive Vice-President and Vice-President for Academic Affairs. He was Director of The University of Texas at Austin's former Division of Natural Resources and Environment. He served as President of The University of Texas at San Antonio from 1973 to 1977, and was Acting Director of the UT Marine Science Institute from 1978 to 1979. His research interests, widely published, include economic geology and mineral resources, environmental geology, natural resources geology, and the geology of Texas and Mexico.*

I would like to open this discussion with a quotation that came to mind yesterday as Bob Strauss spoke:

"In these days when everyone speaks to his rights and no one speaks to his duties, the linkages of society are loosened. Vice and crime have multiplied. And if the memory of our heroic days had not stopped the Republic at the very edge of the precipice, it would have surely perished."

That's a translation of words spoken 150 years ago, in 1828, by Simon Bolivar, the great liberator of South America, as he fought to hold together the separate states in what would have been, had he succeeded, a United States of

133

South America.

Now, 150 years later, we, too, hear more of right and less of duty; we, too, have a memory of heroic days. The panels that preceded this one focused on rationale and priorities: rationale for a new partnership between business, government, and labor; priorities that must be considered in establishing such a partnership.

**Conference Themes**

The necessity, indeed the urgency, for establishing an effective business-labor-government partnership was established by our keynote speaker and followed up in the first panel discussion. Felix Rohatyn mentioned "political impotence and bureaucratic ineptitude"; he called for new structures or new institutions; and he presented several New York models of such new structures and institutions for illustration.

The second panel identified for us a number of priorities for the new partnership's attention: (1) decreasing what has become excessive destructive regulation; (2) improving our capabilities for capital formation; (3) increasing productivity; and (4) examining the areas of energy, inflation, unemployment, and export policy.

In the discussion pursued by the priorities panel, additional fundamental priorities emerged. Mr. Swearingen said the need to establish a basis for partnership requires defining and reexamining the kind of government we want— an equal partnership, or one in which government will inevitably be the senior partner. What kind of partnership will it be?

---

"What stands in the way of coming to the new partnership, to the new structures, to the new institutions, that are so urgently needed? What must be done to overcome these barriers? Are the barriers attitudinal? Do they stem from a factionalized society, a house divided among many issues and divided ideologically? Are the barriers statutory? Is it, in fact, against the law to form a new government-labor-business partnership? If so, what laws stand in the way?

Peter Flawn
UT Austin

Bill Coors suggested that our first priority must be to correct gross misconceptions about the U.S. economic system, to promote a favorable attitude permitting a partnership between business and government. Consideration of attitude brings us very nicely to the business of this panel, an examination of barriers.

What stands in the way of coming to the new partnership, to the new structures, to the new institutions that are so urgently needed? What must be done to overcome these barriers? Are the barriers attitudinal? Do they stem from a factionalized society, a house divided among many issues and divided ideologically? Are the barriers statutory? Is it, in fact, against the law to form a new government-labor-business partnership? If so, what laws stand in the way?

To borrow the title from Walt Rostow's book, the task of this panel is "Getting There from Here." What are the fundamental barriers? How can they be overcome?

*The next panel follows Donald Rice's presentation of two points: one, the question is no longer whether some degree of business-government cooperation is desirable, but whether we can achieve the proper degree of cooperation, given our present institutions; and, two, society as a whole must agree to goals and trade-offs in order to solve pressing problems.*

*Harvey Kapnick specifically reemphasizes what seems to be coming out of the conference as a whole: the need for proper costing of political and social decisions. Ira Millstein, who has been involved in the tedious process of making regulatory agencies work better, vividly relates what is involved. Mr. Millstein argues that reform depends on considering whether the agency is needed at all, and on generating alternative ways of achieving social ends. He also remarks that "the great debate is forming" regarding the role of the Presidency in relation to regulatory agencies and in the setting of national goals.*

*Taking up a theme begun in the first panel discussion, Joseph Swidler argues that the emergence of single issue voting groups may be one of the crucial developments of our time.*

*These insightful panelists bring to a head many of the viewpoints of the preceding sections and help set the tone for section four's task of wrapping up the conference.*

**Harvey Kapnick**
*Chief Executive Officer,*
Arthur Andersen & Company

*Harvey Kapnick is Chairman of the Board and Chief Executive Officer of Arthur Andersen & Co., certified public accountants. He is a graduate of Cleary College and the University of Michigan Graduate School of Business Administration. He serves on the State Department's Advisory Committee on Transnational Enterprises, and is Chairman of its Subcommittee on International Accounting Standards. He was appointed by the President to serve on the Advisory Committee on Trade Negotiations. Mr. Kapnick has contributed his time to universities (including Duke, Stanford, and the University of Chicago), to cultural enterprises (including the Chicago Symphony and Chicago Lyric Opera), and to nonprofit organizations (the United Way, the Red Cross, the American Cancer Society, and the Rehabilitation Institute of Chicago).*

## Entering a New Era

The old saying, "There's not much new," is applicable here: many of the barriers have been covered already. Still I would like to refocus our thinking a little bit on three or four very basic issues.

Looking at it as an outsider, the question you really have to ask first is, "Why are we here?" I'm not sure this question has been addressed as much as I would like in a symposium like this.

During my lifetime we have gone through two major eras in the United States. The first era was focused on national defense: winning a very important war, bringing the country, and the world, through that war.

137

The second era is best summed up in our concern with social issues. Those social issues, except for our distraction over Vietnam and Watergate, have really been the main focus of the country in the past two decades. Looking at these two eras, we see there was one thing that was always given: We were a great nation. We thought that we could stay economically strong merely because of that greatness. As I see it, the reason we're here today is that we have entered a new era, even though many people may not yet have recognized that era and its problems.

This coming era has got to center on this issue: can we remain economically strong? Because if we can't remain economically strong, then we are going to have, as a nation, some very serious social problems. These problems may even extend to events like you see in other countries, armed demonstrations and so forth. The overriding issue is economic strength.

I would like to use the old example: the richer you are, the less you need to balance your checkbook. You can go on for years without balancing the checkbook. But some of us who come from very meager backgrounds learned very early in life that you have to keep that checkbook in balance. Throughout the last several decades we have not zeroed in on keeping it in balance.

The real reason we're here is that we are entering a new era. We've got to agree, as a nation, that our main focus should be on remaining economically strong. Some delays that you've seen—the delay in balancing our trade budgets, delays in balancing our fiscal budgets, delays in establishing priorities—all have to lead you to the conclusion that this overriding issue of strength in our economy has just not been agreed upon.

### Barriers to Partnership—Attitudes

I see three basic issues, as far as barriers are concerned. The first issue has been discussed at some length; Peter Flawn touched upon it, and so did Don Rice. This is the issue of attitude. In many ways, we have a great asset in being a very large nation. The vastness of our nation has led us to develop agricultural and industrial might over the years. But the vastness of our country also helps create many of the divisive issues.

One area of the country is more interested in one particular issue, another area in another issue. Bob Strauss, I know, has experienced this while trying to balance off the "GAP Treaty." How do you make trade-offs among all of these various factions? Here in this symposium we've talked about environment, we've talked about various issues. How do we balance these? We've got to look at how to maintain some sort of a cohesive attitude. I would like to see a cohesive attitude toward improving our economic strength.

Another thing bothers me on attitudinal issues. We hear so much about one factional issue, the overriding issue to that particular group. Many of these groups, I suggest, are as much self-interest groups as they are public interest groups. We have come to think of some of those who espouse one social issue as a public interest group. But they are looking out as much for their personal bias and self-interest as any other group in our nation. We have to recognize this.

On the other hand, I think that business also has created some of these attitudinal problems. One of the main barriers to the solution to some of the problems is the lack of agreement on what the role of the corporation really is. Some of you who may not be as close to corporate life as others probably don't realize it, but there is no uniform agreement among the leadership in business concerning the role of the corporation.

Some believe that the only role is to make profits. But the more learned and enlightened leaders of our business community, I believe, have changed that attitude in the last few years. Businessmen realize that they have a broader role today. They have a duty to their employees: to try to help

---

**"Some of you who may not be as close to corporate life as others probably don't realize it, but there is no uniform agreement among the leadership in business concerning the role of the corporation."**

them in the communities in which they live and in which they have factories and plants.

Every person in the nation works for one of three groups: either for business; for government; or for the non-profit institutions. The biggest sector is industry. Business has to do a better job of educating employees. Every employee is accessible.

Many of us have not done the job of identifying what business is all about: why we need profits, what our concern is with social issues. I do not know many business leaders today who aren't as much concerned with the environment as most of those who are in many of the public interest groups.

The question is: how far do you go and what's the timing? That's the issue. It's not whether or not we should have clean air or clean water. Too many businessmen are still afraid to get involved in politics. This is natural. They have come up playing a very different role. Yet most of us today realize that the business sector has got to get involved in politics. I hope they never get involved so much that they take over the institutions, as Don Rice suggests. Business should stay in a very neutral role as far as some issues are concerned.

Another facet on the business side of barriers to partnership is the role of the chief executive. The chief executives of many of our major corporations are still tied down to the day-to-day running of the corporate enterprise. They must look to assuming a much broader role. Running the business is obviously their number-one priority, but they also must be organized so that they can participate at a very high level in all parts of the government.

**Structures**

Don Rice pointed out that the structural issue goes back twenty years—to when we evolved the concept of the independent agency. The independent agency today, in my

---

"The question is: how far do you go and what's the timing? That's the issue. It's not whether or not we should have clean air or clean water."

judgment, is the problem. We've got to have some new institutions, as Don Rice indicated. Why?

We now have two types of law in this country: those passed by our legislatures and those created by our government structures. I don't think there is anyone in this room who would deny that once the government has passed a law we citizens should obey that law. The issue, however, is that the second type of law, which has equal force with any laid down by the Congress, is now overrunning the country.

When Congress passes a law, it trades off priorities. When individual agencies pass a regulation, they never trade off priorities. They look at the very narrow issues of their own agencies. It's that type of law that must be either overcome or organized in some new institutional structure so that we can get a handle on it.

## Financial Accounting

The last issue I would like to zero in on, since I'm an accountant by background, is that of financial facts. Maybe one of the most fundamental barriers to a working relationship among various factions, business and labor and all the others, is in the sector of public information. We really have no hard financial facts.

Just as an illustration: some of you read the papers and you see that the deficit this coming year is going to be $30 billion. I question that. Not because it's not going to be thirty billion—but let us look at the facts. The facts are that some of the agencies are not included in the unified budget. So you have off-balance-sheet financing and off-balance-sheet costs. Industry had that type of financial reporting twenty years ago. Congress and the Security Exchange Commission made them clean it up, so that now, when you look at a corporate financial statement, it is all there. But in government you don't have that.

Secondly, the deficit is figured on a cash basis. Any accountant knows cash basis provides the easiest way in the world to fudge the numbers. The reason you can fudge the numbers with a cash-basis financial statement is that you stop paying bills, or you pay more bills, so that you play around with those numbers. And you don't need to recognize future liabilities.

Let me give you one little number. We talk about a $30 billion deficit this year. And yet, if you look at some of the consolidated financial statements the government has started on a prototype basis, the noncash charge this past year for unfunded social security was $172 billion. That is a type of accrual accounting. I'm not saying it should be funded. I'm not saying in this case $172 billion is the number. But the truth is, we do not have good solid facts.

Another important issue is that when you come to financial facts and get involved in trade-offs you get numbers which support one person's point of view. So as long as you're arguing those sets of financial facts, obviously they are biased. Some way has to be found to bring better facts to the debate.

I would like to point out that the Business Round Table (it will be announced within the next month) has actually undertaken to identify the excess cost of some government regulations for six major agencies of the federal government. Our firm happens to be making this long study. To my knowledge, this is the first time major facts on individual regulations have ever been brought to bear on the debate on regulations.

I would like to make one closing remark. Being in a partnership myself and saying "this is a partnership" intrigues me. In my firm we have over a thousand partners. I have to deal with partners every day, and everyone thinks they own the whole thing. And they do. So it's very difficult, from a management standpoint.

Because I deal with a thousand partners, I was impressed with George Kozmetsky's opening remarks yesterday. If you're going to have a true partnership, you must learn to listen. We've never learned to listen to the other person's

---

**"In my firm we have over a thousand partners. I have to deal with partners every day, and everyone thinks they own the whole thing. And they do. So it's very difficult, from a management standpoint."**

point of view—that may well be one of the most difficult barriers to overcome. People who have very definite points of view, including myself, normally don't like to listen.

**Ira Millstein**
Partner,
Weil, Gotshal and Manges

*Ira Millstein is a New Yorker, a graduate of Columbia University School of Engineering and School of Law. He is a partner in the law firm of Weil, Gotshal and Manges. His Washington service includes work in the Antitrust Division of the Department of Justice and the Office of Price Stabilization. He has extensive experience in the areas of economic regulation and rate making, trade, consumer finance, and energy. He has long been involved with his alma mater, Columbia University, with the American Bar, the New York State Bar, the City of New York Bar Association, and the City of New York itself.*

The fundamental barrier to cooperation at this point is that mechanically the system isn't working. I understand problems of attitude and so on, but mechanically the system doesn't work. We have a fourth branch of government, the administrative and regulatory agencies, which has grown geometrically to accomplish a whole lot of social goals we all want.

We have hundreds of these agencies scattered around the country doing their job with intense singlemindedness. Why don't they work better? How can we make them work better? How can government and industry work together if the whole system doesn't function right?

And it's true the system isn't functioning right. Mechanically, these regulatory agencies don't operate in a way to encourage business to participate, don't work in a way to encourage the public to participate, don't work in a way to encourage the interest groups to participate.

As a result, the conflict that Don Rice was talking about exists. Everybody would find a quick shot that's going to make the regulatory agencies turn around and function beautifully and have everything go right. Just a quickie, one global idea that's going to solve the whole problem.

I want to assure you there isn't any such global idea anywhere around. As a lawyer, I look at myself as a sort of mechanic. I don't describe legalization as increasing red tape at all. I describe legalization as finding solutions. In a number of respects we lawyers have been charged with finding solutions.

I'm a member of the American Bar Association's Commission on the Law in the Economy. We spent two years writing this book about steps to be taken to achieve better functioning of this regulatory system. I was appointed by the President to the Administrative Conference of the United States, with the charge of making the regulatory system work better.

One problem is, nobody in this room ever heard of the ABA Commission's report. If you did hear about it, you wouldn't take the trouble to read it. You probably don't know what the Administrative Conference of the United States *is*, even though it was created by Congress and appointed by the President. It's working hard, quietly, under a big black blanket which nobody ever picks up, to ask: How do you make this thing work better? Well, what's the problem?

It's this: The way you're going to make these agencies work better will consist of possibly fifty or a hundred different ideas, all of which will have to be slowly implemented, imposed, and adopted by the agencies as we all pound away at them, and at ourselves, to make the system

---

"Everybody would find a quick shot that's going to make the regulatory agencies turn around and function beautifully and have everything go right. Just a quickie, one global idea that's going to solve the whole problem. I want to assure you there isn't any such global idea anywhere around."

function better. The problem with administrative reform, with this tremendous barrier of a malfunctioning system, is that it's difficult. It's complex. It's not going to be easy. It requires a hundred different approaches. And most important, it's dull as hell.

If I try to describe what you have to do to overcome the barrier of a malfunctioning administrative process, I know you're all going to go to sleep. It reminds me of Shapiro's Law: In New York, if you have to explain it already, it's no good.

### Administrative Reform

I'm going to violate Shapiro's Law. I hope you'll stay with me just for a few minutes as I run through some of the things that have to be done to make the process work better. One or two of them might stimulate your interest. Number one: In looking at administrative reform, you have to start with the question, do you need it in the first place? Why do we have the agency? That takes the absolute topmost place. And we're in the process of doing that. Mr. Swidler has been involved in this process for a long time. It's happening all around us. We're looking at a lot of our regulatory effort and saying, "Do we need the agency? Shouldn't we maybe remit this sector of the economy back to the market place?"

After all the talking, we did it in one place, the airlines. We've remitted airlines back to the market place as best we can. We've taken it out from under regulation and put it back to the forces of the market economy. It seems to be working. We'll see. We don't really know what the end result will be. It looks good for a year or so. But who knows what's going to happen down the line? Now, we ought to be subjecting every element of the system to that same analysis.

---

**"The problem with administrative reform, with this tremendous barrier of a malfunctioning system, is that it's difficult. It's complex. It's not going to be easy. It requires a hundred different approaches. And most important, it's dull as hell."**

We ought to be looking at the Interstate Commerce Commission, and the Security Exchange Commission, the other regulatory agencies which are gatekeepers to let you in or out of an industry or set rates. We ought to be seeing whether those gatekeepers ought to stay in existence, or whether we ought to put them out of business and let the industry go back to competition. Will competition work better?

The fundamental premise of this society is that competition is the great governor of the market place. We ought to be looking all the time to see whether or not we picked the right method for regulation. Maybe we ought to get rid of it. Maybe we ought to change it. There is nothing sacrosanct. That's the beginning of the analysis.

The second part of the analysis is to look for alternatives. We don't have to use the tried-and-true method of mandated types of regulation. We can use tax incentives and other forms of regulation, to encourage the industry through incentives while permitting it to remain basically unregulated by law.

There are all sorts of good ideas floating around at the moment. We ought to be looking for ways to substitute for the old forms, and bring in new forms which are less expensive and have a way of putting the burden back on industry to get the job done itself, rather than being told specifically what to do.

After deciding whether or not we need it in the first place, we then look for more intelligent mechanisms for doing it. Let's take a look into the agencies which are already in business. What can we do there? There we have a tremendous task of balancing. As Don Rice said, we have a whole lot of national goals, all of which are competing with one another: check inflation, encourage growth, reduce unemployment, ensure national security, clean up the

---

"The fundamental premise of this society is that competition is the great governor of the market place. We ought to be looking all the time to see whether or not we picked the right method for regulation."

environment, improve energy efficiency. Well, how can anybody do all of that at once? You can't. How do you balance all of these things?

There are a lot of different ways of doing it. Everybody agrees the balancing has to be done. Nobody is fighting the issue of whether or not to balance national interests and the tasks of the agencies. But how do you do it? That is some kind of job. It isn't anything that you just quickly say, well, the President ought to be the one to step in and do the balancing and call the shots.

**The President's Role**

There are immense constitutional issues about the President of the United States marching in and stating that the Environmental Protection Agency's cotton-dust regulation is no good. He was taken to court the next day. There's a problem about the President stepping in and saying strip-mining regulations issued by the Department of the Interior are too onerous, we can't have them in this energy-necessary era. He was taken to court the next day.

How do you get the President involved? It's easy to say the President should be involved, but it's awful hard to do. We have to be ingenious about finding ways to get the Executive into the process of balancing.

The best minds in the country ought to go to work on this question, figuring out who is going to do the balancing and who is going to check the balancer. What if we don't like the way the President comes out in his balancing process? Supposing the President decides, well, we really have one major problem, and that's inflation. And all the rest of it goes away. And I don't care that the Environmental Protection

---

"We have a whole lot of national goals, all of which are competing with one another: check inflation, encourage growth, reduce unemployment, ensure national security, clean up the environment, improve energy efficiency. Well, how can anybody do all of that at once? You can't. How do you balance all of these things?"

Agency wants to clean up the ozone or the water or whatever—we can't afford it this year. No further activity. Congress comes along and says, wait a minute. That wasn't our rule. Our rule was clean water, clean air, clean ozone, et cetera. Well, now, who is going to make that decision when the two of them are at loggerheads? Are we going to have to wait for the next election? I'm not quite sure. This is not an easy job. Both the Congress and the President have a clear role to play in the balancing process, and nobody has yet spelled out who belongs where.

The great debate is forming. Everybody in the country ought to be participating in debating the question of Presidential and Congressional authority. It's probably one of the most interesting issues this government has ever faced, a brand new issue in 1979, one that's got to be confronted and solved. How do you balance? Sure we want to balance, but how do you do it. Another balancing question, cost-benefit.

**What Is Cost-Benefit?**

When Congress passes a law saying clean up the environment, does that mean at any cost, or is the agency involved supposed to decide on what the cost-benefit analysis is? Namely, how much money should we spend to accomplish what? At what point does the spending of money outweigh the good that we're going to accomplish?

Do we want our agencies to engage in that process? I think so. I think we want every agency that's got a social responsibility to pick up and look at the cost-benefit before they undertake the job of whatever it is they're doing, whether it's safety, health, social benefit, or whatever it is. The agency ought to know how much it's going to spend to get it done and whether or not the expected benefit is worth it. We agree that ought to be done. Somebody ought to think about it.

---

**"The great debate is forming. Everybody in the country ought to be participating in debating the questions of Presidential and Congressional authority."**

But who is going to make the decision of what the cost-benefit risk is? Who will decide how much should be spent to accomplish what degree of good? It's fine to talk about cost-benefit analysis. It would be wonderful even if we could conduct a real cost-benefit analysis. Can we assume we have a method of deciding what the cost-benefit is? For example, we don't have such a method in such things as life. How much is a life worth? How much are we willing to spend for safety? These are questions we don't even know how to begin to answer yet, so how can we implement a cost-benefit analysis? Yet we have to if we're going to be imposing social, safety, health regulations on the country.

**Who Makes the Decisions?**

But assuming we know how to do that, who is going to call that shot? Who is going to make the decision that, all right, you've just passed the point of no return. Don't spend any more money to save another life. Don't spend any more money to clean up the air that much more. Is it the President? Is it Congress? Is it the agency itself? Should there be checks and balances one on the other? If we are going to encumber the system with this analysis, then the decision of who ultimately makes the decision must be faced. Or we will fall of our own weight in a new administrative process. Again, here is a very important balancing aspect in government which we don't know how to do.

We need to get on about the business of deciding how we're going to balance risks and who is going to make the final determination. Will it be the President? Congress? Both of them? And what are the mechanics that we're going to use to accomplish that? We don't know how.

I find a fundamental barrier to be that in the year 1979, recognizing all these problems, we still don't know how to do these things. And we had better start paying attention to the debate that's coming concerning how to do it.

I just picked out of the DDR the other day a hearing on ozone before Senator Muskie where these issues were crystallized. In came Messrs. Shultze and Kahn to talk about the fact that it was getting too expensive to clean up the ozone. On the other side was Douglas Costle, whom you heard earlier, plus some environmental groups, saying, well, nobody told us to worry about how much it was going to cost to clean up the ozone. Congress's directive was, "Clean it up no matter what the cost is."

The inflation fighters came in and said, "No, that wasn't the directive. We've got to have other goals and it's costing too much. Don't do it this year. Wait until next year."

Senator Muskie sat there scratching his head and saying, "Well, really, who's right and how do we make that decision? Is that my job or the President's job? I would really like him to keep his nose out of that," said Muskie, "and yet, on the other hand, I don't see any power in Congress's hands to do anything about it." And there we had the collision, and a lot of confused hearings, and nobody knew exactly what to do. And away they went with no resolution. So here we are in 1979. These problems are confronting us, and nobody has the plumbing to deal with them.

## Management Procedures

The ultimate in boredom in regulatory reform is improving procedures in management. Everybody knows that the administrative process is slow. It's costly; it's cumbersome. Yes, there the lawyers do have a problem. It's true, in the early days of administrative reform or in the early days of creating these agencies, we argued we wanted something like the judicial process imposed on these agencies.

Well, if every agency that's having a hearing has to be a little courtroom with witnesses and cross-examination and arguments and appeals, nothing is ever going to get done. It only took us about thirty-five years to find that out. But we

---

"We need to get on about the business of deciding how we're going to balance risks and who is going to make the final determination. Will it be the President? Congress? Both of them? And what are the mechanics that we're going to use to accomplish that? We don't know how."

151

found it out, and now we're saying, "Well, we're going to have new procedures."

Okay. What are the new procedures? A notice and comment. We won't have witnesses. You'll just come in and tell us what you think and we'll listen. And then if we find disputed issues of fact we'll have a hearing, and only on those little issues of fact will we have cross-examination and so on. It sounds easy to do that. Not one agency in the United States government has been able to get itself on track into that new procedure. Why? Because nobody is hitting them on the head; nobody is pushing them.

Although there's an Administrative Conference of the United States, do you realize there is no inspector general of all these agencies, all these hundreds of agencies? They all do what they want, and there isn't anybody telling them, "Your procedures are rotten; you oughtn't have a trial-type proceeding. You ought to have a notice and hearing, and if you don't, we're going to cut off your funding." Nobody ever says that. So each agency rolls along doing its own trick, having its own hearings, developing its own procedures. Nobody mushes them together and hits them on the head and makes them straighten out.

There ought to be somebody around in Washington whose function it is to go around these agencies and publicize their deficiencies, not their merits. Nobody wants to interfere with the goals they've been set up to meet; but criticize them about the way they go about their business. That's where your money is getting lost in large quantities. That's where the hearings are not taking place. That's where the public is not getting in. That's where industry is not being heard. Because the sheer act of getting before the agency to tell them what's bothering you is so cumbersome, so costly, most

---

"There ought to be somebody around in Washington whose function it is to go around these agencies and publicize their deficiencies, ... criticize them about the way they go about doing their business.... Because the sheer act of getting before the agency ... is so cumbersome, so costly, most people walk away bored."

people walk away bored. They would rather not wait to get in there, and they just ignore the whole procedure.

So we've got to find a way to grease the skids, so to speak, make it work. Make the system function through procedures and management. Force advance planning. Force policy planning. Force the correction of silly procedures. And make it happen.

**Sunset**

Last, but not least, and this is interesting because nobody knows how to do it: Sunset. You've all heard about Sunset. What's Sunset? Well, does every regulatory effort that was put on the books deserve to stay there forever? Don't some outlive their usefulness? Does every law that Congress passes creating a new agency, and the agency it creates, deserve to stay there forever? Or was it created to fill a need?

Maybe the agency is now looking around for new things to do because it has a $50 million budget, and it's doing things that Congress never dreamed it was going to do. Why? Simply because they're there. Agencies have a way of filling vacuums, and if they haven't got a function to perform any more, they find new functions to perform.

Sunset simply means let's take a look, on a regular basis, at every regulatory initiative we ever undertook in this country, and see whether or not it still is necessary, required, or whether it ought to just be eliminated. That's all it means. The states are doing it already.

Here is an area where many state governments have got the beat on the federal government. Sunset is quite an accepted thing in about half the states. Gradually, one at a time, or three at a time, or four—it's nothing you can do very

---

"So we've got to find a way to grease the skids, so to speak, make it work. Make the system function through procedures and management. Force advance planning. Force policy planning. Force the correction of silly procedures. And make it happen."

dramatically. You can't do them all at once, because there are so many of them, but you pick them out in an order of priority and you start looking at each of the regulatory initiatives you've undertaken, to see which you can keep, which you can modify, which you can terminate.

You simply do not operate on the theory that because you once created a regulatory initiative, it must be forever. Some of them have outlived their usefulness. In the process, if you hit one or two and get rid of them, you've accomplished something.

Not only should that be done with respect to the Congressional initiatives (laws), but each agency ought to do likewise. Think of some of the areas like the Federal Trade Commission. Think of the number of rules and regulations which over the years the Federal Trade Commission, the Security Exchange Commission, have issued. The books are full of them. Do they all still mean anything? I don't know. I don't think the agency knows. Does anybody really read them any more? Does anybody know what all those rules and regulations are? Are they still all applicable? Are some of the industries to which they apply even in existence?

When we studied the Federal Trade Commission and looked at some wool labeling and textile regulations that had been issued in the '30s, we found that the industries to which they applied no longer existed. Yet there was a bureau in the Federal Trade Commission that was enforcing these regulations with respect to industries which no longer exist. So we suggested that we eliminate the Wool, Textile, and Fiber Bureau. Well, it was eliminated. And you know what? Nothing happened. It was fine. The world survived.

These are the kind of silly little things you have to do to achieve administrative reform. We have to get focused on the plumbing. I think the ideas are important. Getting it done is more important. It's dull and complex, but it's worthy of everybody's time because this is where the reform is going to come from.

**Joseph Swidler**
*Partner,*
Leva, Hawes, Symington,
Martin and Oppenheimer

*Joseph Swidler was born in Chicago and was educated at the University of Illinois, the University of Florida, and the University of Chicago. He now practices law as a partner in the firm of Leva, Hawes, Symington, Martin and Oppenheimer. He served as a solicitor in the Department of the Interior, as an attorney for the Tennessee Valley Authority, and as Tennessee Valley Authority's General Counsel. He was a member of the staff of Assistant Secretary of the Navy Forestal, and later served on the War Production Board. He was appointed to the New York State Public Service Commission by Governor Rockefeller, and as Chairman of the Federal Power Commission by President Kennedy. He is now an adviser to the Electric Power and Gas Research Institute.*

Reform isn't one thing, but many things, and we're going to have to work on all of them. In the study made by the National Science Foundation, referred to by Peter Flawn, we identified a dozen barriers to government-business cooperation: The Freedom of Information Act requirements, which make it very difficult for people to submit their confidential material, knowing that anyone can retrieve it; the Sunshine Laws, which put any participant in an advisory committee in the position of having any indiscretion exposed to his competitors in the world; conflict of interest requirements; protection of proprietary information and patent rights; an enormous amount of red tape.

If you want to have a partnership in a research program or a development program, problems with the annual

155

appropriation process must be resolved. The instability of the programs, the fact that faces keep changing on the other side, makes it necessary to reeducate the chiefs of the bureaus and the people you're working with, because they don't stay very long. There are antitrust hazards if more than one company in an industry is required in a cooperative program.

Is there something common to all of these individual problems?

### Dominant Historical Forces

In most periods, it's hard for people who are undergoing the traumas of the time to recognize the dominant historical forces which are determining the direction of social movement. Historians found, hundreds of years later, that crucial changes in world history were due to such things as the deep plow, gunpowder, armor, the development of the stirrup, which made it possible for a horseman to use the power of the horse in addition to his own strength in wielding a lance. These turned out to be revolutionary forces. Some of these underlying forces are working in our own society; perhaps if we could identify them it would be easier to know what to do about them.

I do have some suspicions; I think there's a pretty good chance that the development of single-issue voting groups may be one of the crucial developments of our time, and that history will record President Carter as the first to understand and make effective use of single-issue voting blocks.

The demand of people in many places for a direct voice in the political decisions, what is called participatory democracy, is another great turning point in the way our system functions. Participatory democracy is made possible by all the developments in transportation and communication. The art of polling, for example, so that people in office are told what to do as they read the Gallup and other

---

"In most periods, it's hard for people who are undergoing the traumas of the time to recognize the dominant historical forces which are determining the direction of social movement."

polls. This problem will perhaps come to even greater dimensions when two-way TV makes it possible to get instant opinions on any problem from everyone who owns a TV set.

I think there has been a great decline in the individual discretion allowed the people we elect to office. Elected officials have become mouthpieces rather than leaders. Or at least the problems of leadership, of asserting a goal that goes beyond the general public understanding, have become more and more difficult.

We are now testing our country's ability to manage its affairs under a system which approaches the town-hall conception of democracy, with everyone voting on every issue and asserting a right of veto over social decisions. The polls, the referenda, the letter-writing campaigns, the direct intervention in administrative and judicial proceedings, have all had a great impact on how the decisions are made.

These speculations apply to the subject we are discussing today: how we get from here to there. The problems we face have been brilliantly dissected. But how we move to reform, and particularly how we create the climate of opinion in which reform can flourish, is a crucial question. We find very little support for solutions of compromise. There are very few voices speaking for the need for trade-offs—another way of saying the overall public interest, or the benefit-cost solution. They all come to the same thing.

Apparently, compromise doesn't win voters or even sell newspapers. We find our major organs of opinion as dedicated to the support of particular single-issue objectives as the leaders of some of the single-issue organizations themselves.

We face many centrifugal forces in our society. But there are some centripetal values as well. For instance, the desire of everyone to have a bigger overall pie that we can divide so

---

"Elected officials have become mouthpieces rather than leaders. Or at least the problems of leadership, of asserting a goal that goes beyond the general public understanding, have become more and more difficult."

that all of us can live better without living at the expense of others. We can build, but we are going to have to have someone speaking for the center instead of for the extremes.

We are going to have to have a better understanding that you can't accommodate all the demands of all the special-interest groups. Ira Millstein spoke eloquently on that subject. I don't think there is a general public understanding. Not all of the members of these special-interest groups are immune to reason. The members of labor unions, the members of the Sierra Club, the members of the Business Round Table, all are capable of adjusting to a trade-off policy, and to the necessity for compromise. But the voices for that kind of leadership have been very muted.

What we hear are the voices of the demonstrators, the people who label their opponents the "Dirty Dozen" on the basis of voting on a single issue, the people who take a position one way or another on the abortion question, which is their only interest as they go to the polls.

**Donald Rice**
*RAND Institute*

**Benefit/Benefit Trade-Offs**
Institutional reform is badly and widely needed. I don't believe for an instant that, if you look forward a couple of decades, we will see a time in which there is less regulatory activity than there is today. But we can find ways to do it more effectively, to bring about different forms through which it's done, to organize it better, or whatever, to see that better decisions are made.

The hard, tough job of institutional reform is before us, and we don't know enough about it. Several members of the panel commented on that. Such reform ought to be high on the agenda of every organization in the country, every group in the country, every individual in the country interested in public policy and in public affairs. Certainly that ought to be true of our schools of public affairs and our research institutes working on those problems.

The question of benefit-cost considerations of trade-offs is extraordinarily important. We want to be careful about how we proceed and how we view all that. We don't want to get drawn into asking our leaders to make direct judgments of how many dollars we ought to pay for some particular benefit that is incommensurate with dollar tags. Dollars are only, in that calculus, being used as a measure of the resources that have to be put in to produce a particular level of benefit.

We're interested in things like finding out if it takes X dollars to get 95 percent of the job done, and two or three X more to get the last five percent done. In a sense, we're really interested in benefit-benefit comparisons. We're facing limited ability in what we can do, we have limited resources to spread among all these objectives, and we need to understand that kind of calculus in order to make sensible trade-offs of the sort we've been talking about.

I suggested we think about assigning more responsibilities to the President for taking the lead in setting these kinds of trade-off. I made that suggestion with considerable trepidation. People like Senator Muskie wouldn't like that idea. He would prefer to keep more direct control over the baby that he helped give birth to.

People in the country today are concerned about whether the President—not only the current incumbent but other recent occupants—hasn't found it difficult enough carrying out the current set of responsibilities. Two thoughts in response to that concern: one, you ought to consider that the current alternative is to have that individual's appointees implementing the same laws and pursuing the same objectives, but doing it in a largely uncoordinated way. And, second, I for one can't find anybody else who sits in a position that might speak for the center, as was said earlier, or who can compare the benefit here to the benefit there, and make these kinds of trade-offs that need to be made.

**Harvey Kapnick**
*Arthur Andersen & Co.*

I would agree with ninety percent of what Don Rice says except for one thing. We have to be careful in this cost-benefit analysis because you can't quantify, in most cases,

159

benefits. You can quantify the costs, but the quantification of the benefits is a very difficult thing. Maybe one of the big failures is that nobody really wants to zero in on making that decision when you're talking about life and death.

When you're talking about whether we want clean air, obviously we all want clean air; but it's the degree. Now the unfortunate thing today is not that the decisions are wrong; it's the failure to make decisions. In other words, as I think Ira Millstein mentioned concerning the Senator Muskie hearing, somebody within the nation has to make those decisions. They're tough decisions, but they have to be made if we're going to balance them off. If we aren't going to balance them off, then what you've got is an open pocketbook.

*The Moderator observes that he always thought the President appointed the Cabinet officers, who controlled the rule- and regulation-making efforts of the agencies. He asks whether Mr. Millstein is saying that these agencies are responsible to no one.*

### Ira Millstein
*Weil, Gotshal and Manges*

That's right. Let me explain, because it's been an interesting development. Yes, the Cabinet offices run these executive departments. But the problem is that Congress came along and delegated to these very Cabinet officers and their departments new laws to be implemented. This is the whole executive agency.

The Secretary of the Interior has a whole bunch of laws given to him to administer by Congress, not by the President. The issue is, Congress says to the Department of the Interior, "You will make regulations on strip mining according to the following delegation of authority."

The Secretary of the Interior, at that point, has a mandate from Congress to do something—in accordance with very, very broad language. Now, what can he do? He's got to do it.

Congress says, "I told you to do it." Congress says, "I gave you these standards to use."

If the President then moves in on his own department, Congress says, "What are you doing? That's my law he's administering, not yours."

The issue then becomes a solid constitutional one. The only thing we at the ABA could figure out, which saved us, was that, happily, the Constitution of the United States gives the President power to see that the laws of the United States are faithfully executed.

We're trying to stand on that straw to get the President to say, "Well, you know, if the laws are going to be faithfully executed, I can tell him he's doing a bad job, he's really not doing it neatly." Can you imagine it's 1979, and nobody has ever tested how strong that straw is about having laws faithfully executed? That's a constitutional issue.

There have been a few cases, Humphrey's Executor, and so on, but they're not very clear. Most of the cases that went to the Supreme Court had to do with the President's power to remove an appointee to an independent agency who had a term of years and didn't do a good job, and gets fired. Those cases really don't have a lot to do with whether the President can override a strip-mining regulation, an ozone requirement, or cotton-dust regulation. And I must suggest that the constitutional issue is wide open. We don't have a clear picture.


**Joseph Swidler**
*Leva, Hawes, Symington, Martin and Oppenheimer*

Just to add one more element to it, these procedures Congress has prescribed are quasi-judicial procedures; the Secretary is required to make a decision on the record, and then after he looks at the record and is about to make a decision, the President comes along and says, "I want you to do it differently." This is the heart of the problem.

161

### Ira Millstein
*Weil, Gotshal and Manges*

Well, shades of some years ago, with someone in the White House that everybody is nervous about, then you get worried about someone coming in and intervening in activities of the regulatory proceeding. Which really raises the question of whether we should be comfortable at this point with the idea of the President speaking for the center. Yes, he's the one elected official who represents all the people, that's sure, and maybe that gives comfort. But can anyone really understand all the issues that are faced by these regulatory agencies?

I have a feeling that when we opt for the President to solve all these conflicting problems, we're opting for a bygone dream of "Daddy."

I just don't care who the President is, these are monumental problems and are terribly intricate. They involve, in many cases, months, if not years, of hearings by experts; the issue suddenly comes to the top and the President is supposed to step in and reconcile the conflict. How does any one human being do that, and how does any one man get smart enough to solve the wars and the economy and cotton dust all at the same time?

### Exposure and Disclosure

It's a monumentally difficult problem. I would suggest that we ought to take a mini-step before we take a giant step of really delegating to the President a whole bunch of new authority that will probably end his life earlier than otherwise, and that is exposure and disclosure.

One of the steps which the ABA recommended and which the President has come out with is simply asking the agencies to disclose more about what they're doing. If we're really interested in all of this, as we purport to be by holding conferences, maybe what would be good for each of the agencies to do is to publish a regulatory impact statement as the President asked them to do. Just something as simple as that for openers.

What would be a regulatory impact statement? Here is what I've been asked to accomplish; here is the way I'm going about accomplishing it; this is what I think it's going to cost the people who have to comply with it; this is what I think the burden is going to be on the consumer; here are alternate ways which I might have adopted and these are the things I've rejected in favor of what I accepted. Now, that is a regulatory impact statement.

If the Occupational Safety and Health Administration, or the Environmental Protection Agency, or the Energy Research and Development Administration, or whoever, published a statement about everything they were doing, a number of good things would happen. It's almost like disclosure in the corporate area. Once the corporations had the Security Exchange Commission, and once disclosure requirements became more and more intense, corporations behaved better because all of this was going to be public and it was looking over their shoulders.

Maybe agencies and the government could be subjected to exactly the same kind of scrutiny—a Security Exchange Commission for the agencies: disclosure. What are you doing? How much is it going to cost? Who will it hurt? What taxpayers are going to get caught in a blind? How will it impact? Did you think about alternatives? Make them say it out loud and put it someplace where everybody can look, rather than having these decisions happen in a back room, assuming they happen at all.

If they do happen, let's put them out where you can see them. Maybe as a first step that is what we ought to take a look at. Maybe Sunshine for the agencies would be a pretty good thing. If Sunshine is good for business, it might be even better for exposing the way in which the agencies operate and how they come to their decisions. Require them to state what they're doing, and then after a while, after we've seen a little bit of that, maybe we can make a better judgment about who ought to make the final decision.

**Donald Rice**
*RAND Institute*

I'm a great believer in sunlight. I like to live in it, and I think it's also the best disinfectant we know for government activities. Disclosing that kind of information would do an awful lot toward improving the quality of some of the individual decisions made today. Decisions are made within the confines of one or more of the specific separate-issue regulatory agencies that have been set up.

Sunshine doesn't really deal with the larger problem, though, that we're stuck with today. We have these different agencies. Each of them has its own law. Each law is written in such a way that the goals it sets out are declared, implicitly or explicitly, to be paramount and immutable. The agency heads in many cases do not have the authority to take into account the fact that, in pursing their goals, they're causing trouble for somebody else somewhere else. In some cases there is limited authority of that sort; in lots of cases it's just flat ruled out, and that's what some of the disputes have been about when there have been attempts by the President or others to become involved.

We have a situation today in which we're trying to pursue multiple and sometimes conflicting goals. The structure and the law through which we're doing it don't permit trade-offs in many cases. I don't for an instant believe that there's going to be any great success achieved by simply having the President unilaterally and on his own hook try to do more and more of the kind of thing we've been hearing about lately, moving in on this process on his own authority as it exists today.

The Congress, in order to make something like I suggested possible, is going to have to face up to the fact that there is a need for someone somewhere. It's going to be a joint Executive-Legislative procedure of some kind, at least with the Executive proposing and Congress disposing in some way. The latter could be held to some kind of oversight and exception process, rather than having to decide every detail.

Accomplishing valid compromise clearly requires legislative change. But I don't see any other mechanism to get at the larger trade-offs that we all seem to agree need to be handled. I agree they are difficult. I don't know how one person can possibly do all of it in great detail; I assume he wouldn't try. He'd try to work on the more important things. But the problem that we're talking about, by definition, includes or requires going beyond the boundaries of an individual-issue, specific regulatory agency. If you simply look at the organization chart, the next guy above them is the President.

**Joseph Swidler**
*Leva, Hawes, Symington, Martin and Oppenheimer*

The President purported to do something about this. He appointed a coordinating committee of regulators to try to improve the regulatory process. It's significant who he appointed as chairman. What most people were concerned about was the veto power of the Environmental Protection Agency over economic growth, and he appointed Doug Costle the chairman of that group. The President was also quick to assure the environmentalists that he had no intention of applying economic criteria to any environmental laws, and that he was not diluting his support of the environmentalist position one bit.

Turning the problem over to the President without doing something more fundamental in changing public attitudes wouldn't necessarily help.

**Donald Rice**
*RAND Institute*

I would like to see public attitudes come along, too, but the mechanism you suggest clearly isn't working. It runs up against the problem Ira Millstein raised: the authority really isn't there to make it do something that the members don't want to do voluntarily, or feel they can't do within their charter. Costle has clearly been backing away from what he sees as inappropriate intrusion, through that mechanism and others. This backing away seems appropriate to his responsibilities as the laws state them now. I don't tend to have a lot of confidence in that kind of mechanism anyway. I keep a little plaque in my office that says, "God so loved the world He didn't send a committee."

*This panel seems to argue that what business and those who look at issues from a business standpoint can bring to the other sectors of society is the habit of thinking in terms of cost. Businessmen have not been noted for thinking in terms of social cost, which has been considered the province of government, but that seems to be in the process of significant change.*

*The theme stated by voices as diverse as those of Bill Coors, Jack Conway, and Harvey Kapnick reappears: the necessity of considering all the costs of a decision, including the varying costs dictated by the degree of implementation. This notion is a fundamental part of the ongoing debate of this conference.*

### From the Audience:

With reference to Mr. Millstein's suggestion earlier about the need for reform and some type of plumbing mechanism for regulating agencies: recently the country's largest retailer, Sears, Roebuck and Company, threw down the gauntlet to the federal government and said, "We just can't get there from here." What does the panel think the significance of that suit will be, and what impact is it likely to have on future regulatory agencies?

### Ira Millstein
*Weil, Gotshal and Manges*

I want to be extremely careful how I respond, because we represent some retailers—not Sears, but the ABA rules require me to state in advance that I might have a bias in this respect. The suit is very interesting in terms of bringing to the attention of the American public a serious problem: namely, that of equal employment opportunities. The Sears suit says the government had a policy of encouraging the education and development of the white male population for forty years. In the beginning Sears went through a whole series of governmental policies, beginning with Army, Veterans Administration training et cetera, going down the line over a period of thirty-five years demonstrating that the government encouraged the employment and education of white males.

Then, suddenly, the policy changed; and in a historical context, it was a rather sudden change. The government policy changed to encouraging opportunity for females, minorities, blacks, and so on. And Sears said, "You created a white male pool and now you're coming along telling me that I am engaging in an unfair activity because I don't have enough blacks, I don't have enough women, and so on. I want to employ them, but they're not in the pool and it's very difficult."

That was Sears's suit. What they are trying to say is that they don't know how to go about doing what the government is now ordering them to do, and that basically it is the government's fault. As I say, it's an interesting problem and it's an interesting case. But what's the court supposed to do about it? I have a great deal of confidence in my judges and lawyers and so on, but why did that suddenly get to be a problem for the court to deal with? Since it was the President of the United States and the Congress and everybody else who was involved in creating this problem, they've got to solve it. What's the judge going to do, rule the President out of order for having created the Equal Employment Opportunity Commission? Is he going to rule the Equal Employment Opportunity Commission out of order because they're trying to do something that's right and what the country wants to have done now? No, obviously not.

I don't know where the suit is going to go. I think it's an interesting case, but I'm not quite clear how the judge is going to deal with these monumental global problems. Which simply brings me to the other problem: That is, I just don't think you can dump every problem of the country in the courts. I think the courts have a limited function, when it comes down to it. When it comes to these giant global collisions, I don't think the judicial system is equipped for it.

**Joseph Swidler**
*Leva, Hawes, Symington, Martin and Oppenheimer*

I'd like to add that I think the suit is helpful in focusing on the need in the employment area for consideration of trade-offs, even though it may well be dismissed in the courts for lack of an effective remedy. It may help to get Congress to do something about reconciling this welter of demands upon employers to conform with a great body of conflicting requirements. Sears is to be complimented for having brought the suit, risking the public obloquy, et cetera, that might have occurred from it. The suit brings to the country's attention a serious problem: the difficulty of complying with a lot of different regulations with all the good will in the world.

**From the Audience:**

Mr. Kapnick, your profession has gone through a Congressional subcommittee investigation; I think regulation is what's considered and possibly recommended. Now that that investigation is over, what have been the pluses and minuses of that in relation to our topics today?

**Harvey Kapnick**
*Arthur Andersen & Co.*

Well, I think many of my colleagues in the profession would disagree with some of my statements, but the positive issue that came out of the Congressional hearings on the accounting profession was the fact that we had established dialogue with the government concerning what needed to be done. We in the profession are much like the problem that we're talking about today. We were factionalized. One group believed one thing and another group believed another thing, and there was no pressure point on which you could resolve these conflicting points of view. As I said in my testimony, to me the real benefit was not necessarily the reforms that many of us knew had to come out of those hearings, but the fact that we finally had a dialogue going with someone on resolving the issues.

As I see the problem here, in its context, it's one of finding a mechanism, a structure, a new statutory way to resolve these issues. The very significant benefit of those hearings was this shared insight.

**From the Audience:**

I have a question for Mr. Rice. When John Kenneth Galbraith visited The University of Texas campus a year and a half ago, he was told about the existence of the Institute of Constructive Capitalism. He asked if that was an inadvertent admission that there might be destructive capitalism. You mentioned the de facto national planning that exists on different levels of government. Is there an inevitable conflict between the subject of this conference, the partnership between free market sources and the government, and the future of both national planning and a free market system?

**Donald Rice**
*RAND Institute*

The sum total of all of the economic and social regulation the government is involved in today has such a persuasive effect on decisionmaking in the private sector and on the allocation of resources in the society, that it adds up to an uncoordinated, inadvertent kind of national economic planning.

What that really means is that we ought not think of the problem as a partnership between the free enterprise system and the government, because what we really have is a kind of hybrid process at work. It has many of the characteristics that we normally associate with the concept of free enterprise. But we've come to a point in this country, whether we intended to or not, where there's no such thing as an unregulated industry anymore.

There are lots of specific industries that have long been regulated, utilities and airlines, and so on, but we have a situation today of environmental, work-place, health and safety, and all those kinds of regulation. We're in some sense stuck with a partnership whether we like it or not. The question we need to be groping with is how to make that combined hybrid process turn out the results that we're all after, and to do that in some way that's efficient and consistent with economic growth and all the rest of it.

**Ira Millstein**
*Weil, Gotshal and Manges*

The fact that you get married or have a partner or whatever doesn't mean that you stop having a healthy skepticism for your other part, your better half. The fact that we are into this partnership doesn't mean that we aren't or shouldn't continue to be very skeptical of the guy on the other side. That tension is good and healthy and useful. Industry and business ought to be very skeptical of all government, and test it all the time. Government's skepticism of business is also healthy. It doesn't make for any less of a partnership.

**From the Audience:**

When the country was younger, we had very unco-ordinated policies on expenditures. Every agency pretty much cooked its own budget plan for the next year and submitted it to Congress, or rather to a particular committee of Congress, which then approved it. The early battle over the budget happened not long after the turn of the century, and was finally resolved in the early 1920s, with the creation of a federal budget. It wasn't until a couple of years ago that there was a Congressional budget set up parallel to the Bureau of the Budget.

In the regulatory agency area we're now facing something like that. What we need on the Executive side is a kind of a bureau of regulation parallel to the Bureau of the Budget, and on the Congressional side some sort of apparatus similar to the Congressional Budget Office. It's conceivable that on the administrative side, instead of its being the kind of Presidential bureau of the budget, it would be the regulatory agencies themselves that would establish a coordinating body. It's hard to make it neat because some regulation is under the President and some in specific regulatory agencies. But that would not necessarily be an insuperable problem.

Then the kind of back and forth that goes on between the Office of Management and Budget and the Congressional Budget Office would happen in the regulatory field. What would you think of that as an administrative reform?

**Harvey Kapnick**
*Arthur Andersen & Co.*

You've got the seed of what might be a very interesting approach. One of the things I'm troubled about, which you're obviously trying to get at, is that over the years the Congress has really been the place where we've debated priorities and tried to balance off priorities. As I tried to say in my opening remarks, we got into this situation of the independent agency which delegated responsibility—but without assuming control over it.

Now, if you could take something along the lines you mentioned, and each year also produce a budget including what each agency wants to do and what the impact of doing it would be upon the economy, that might be a very interesting approach. Of course, tying it in with the President so the check-and-balance system could work would be a way of starting within the present framework of society. I think it has a lot of merit.

**Peter Flawn**
*The University of Texas at Austin*

There was a companion suggestion made yesterday that perhaps it would be a good idea to establish a regulation court analogous to the tax court, so decisions about the degree of onerousness or the fairness of regulation would be made by someone other than those writing the regulations. I think it was Mr. Swearingen who suggested that.

**Ira Millstein**
*Weil, Gotshal and Manges*

I think that would be terrible.

**Donald Rice**
*RAND Institute*

Without commenting on the regulatory court part, there is an interesting analogy to be drawn here between what was done with the Budget and Accounting Act in 1921 and the problem we have today. Someone once pointed out that in his role as chief budget maker the President plays an important function, a role of "chief clerk" of the administrative side. That is, the President puts together something which then plays a very strong role in setting the agenda for debate for the year. The budget is much more than just a set of decisions about financing programs. The budget process is a mechanism by which many other important policy subjects are debated. Some such mechanism may, in fact, work here.

I do not have much faith that some kind of committee of the regulators would work very well. Though it may be a mechanism you'd want to make a lot of use of, it wouldn't deal with the entire problem, because fundamentally there's still going to have to be someone on the Executive Branch side to get a decision when those folks can't make important trade-offs themselves. At the same time, the mechanism that gets put in place cannot be purely an Executive Branch one; it has to involve the Congress too. We can probably learn more from the budget committee than the Congressional Budget Office. The Congressional Budget Office is really more of a professional staff that analyzes issues for Congress. It does not have the same degree of authority in the Congressional budget process as the Office of Management and Budget has on the Executive side. But between the Congressional Budget Office and the Budget Committee in the two houses, we have models that could be applied in this area.

**Joseph Swidler**
*Leva, Hawes, Symington, Martin and Oppenheimer*

Nothing is more certain than if the lion and the lamb get together to divide up the spoils, the lion is going to get the lion's share. The question is: What makes one of the parties the lion? There's obviously a great difference between public perception of where the line ought to be drawn in balancing the various considerations and the balance as we have been discussing it here.

The fundamental question is: How can the public understanding be improved? Is there something wrong with the information process that leads to such unrealistic expectations and to such unbalanced demands on the Congress and on these agencies? Has the press done its job or has it catered to the extreme, if not fanatical, minorities? How would you expect the public to understand the issues and the need for balance from the kind of television programs upon which many of them rely for their understanding of the current affairs? You can't expect more from the public than its level of appreciation and sophistication warrants.

**From the Audience:**

Interest has been growing recently in injecting Congressional oversight into the regulatory process. Several bills are now being introduced in Congress which would call for the opportunity of a legislative veto of an agency rule. The United States Chamber and the National Association of Manufacturers and the like are supporting such a concept.

**Ira Millstein**
*Weil, Gothal and Manges*

There's nothing new about legislative vetos. The legislative veto is built into over a hundred regulations already. I'm not sure we're moving the ball significantly, but it seems I've heard some of the debate, and the issue is whether this is going to slow down the process, increase its politicalization, or even be an improvement.

If each regulatory effort is going to be subject to hearings and veto over a long period of time, is this going to improve the system? Will it make it work better? I don't know. I'd have to take it up on an issue-by-issue basis. There may be some delegations of authority to agencies so broad that Congress ought to take a look and see what the agency did with the delegation before it becomes law.

Now, there are other delegations which are kind of pinpointed, and the agency ought to be allowed to go on about its business. If Congress is keeping a string on it, there must be another reason for doing so.

**Harvey Kapnick**
*Arthur Andersen & Co.*

Does that get at the problem of the individual agencies? The overriding problem here is coordinating among the agencies. There are no laws that are proposed or pending to get at that problem of coordination between the agencies, are there?

**Ira Millstein**
*Weil, Gotshal and Manges*

Yes. Within about a week or two, certainly by the end of March, the Administration is going to send up its Regulatory Reform Bill. Three or four things are drifting around at the moment. There's a thing called RARG, which is the Regulatory Analysis Review Group. It's hard to pronounce. The Regulatory Analysis Review Group is lodged in the Council on Wage-Price Stability. Its function is to look at regulations as they are about to come out and say "that's too expensive," if that's the case, then run over to get the President to do something. That's happened two or three times.

There's the Council on Wage-Price Stability, which is keeping an inflation watch on all of this; there's the Council of Economic Advisers, which is keeping a big-picture watch on all these regulations; and then there is the Regulatory

Council, which is made up of the regulators themselves who are trying to talk to one another. Under Douglas Costle's leadership, yesterday or the day before yesterday, it published the first regulatory agenda that the country has ever seen. I will vouch that nobody in this room is ever going to look at it, but it's a great step forward.

Why is it a great step forward? Because now each of the agencies involved in the Regulatory Council has published its agenda for the coming year— a very novel thing. You would think somebody would have done that before, but it's unprecedented. Now you can go down to Washington and get a book which will tell you what every significant regulatory agency is going to do next year. Having gotten that you will, of course, go down to Washington frequently to comment on those activities you don't agree with.

The administration bill is going to wrap up all of this and institutionalize it. Presumably, what it will do will be to take RARG and the Regulatory Council and the Administrative Conference and a piece of the Wage-Price Council and a piece of the Consumer Bankers Association and a piece of the National Science Foundation and a piece of the Federal Register—all these pieces that have to do with regulatory reform—and put them into one place. So there will be in the government one place that collects, and has the ability to do something about, regulatory reform effort. That's what's supposed to happen.

None of the bills introduced in Congress by Ribicoff or any of the others who are intensely interested in reform do that yet. Presumably, an effort is going on inside the Office of Management and Budget right now to pull this stuff together and put it in one place to provide a focal point for administrative reform.

The answer to your question is here, if the Administration goes forward with its plans there will be a required place where these agencies get together and talk to one another, publish agendas, and try to coordinate among themselves.

Douglas Costle said his view was that the cooperation of the regulators is this regulatory reform movement is a must. While I didn't think that was right a year ago, I'm convinced now. They're in existence, and to say we're going to tell them what to do is nonsense.

We've got to make the agencies themselves want reform; and that's not so easy. In any event, everybody is now convinced that it's not a question of laying down the law and telling these people what you've got to do. You've got to get them involved in the game and tell them they're going to have a piece of it, and institutionalize their function.

**Donald Rice**
*RAND Institute*

I hope that the Administration's package does not include a provision for Congressional veto on a detailed regulation-by-regulation basis. Maybe the Congress will insist on having something like that as part of the package before it finishes with it, but that certainly is going to have the effect of dragging out the time associated with getting any particular regulation settled one way or the other. And it involves the Congress in an awful lot of detailed administrative stuff that probably isn't its strong suit.

But we'll just have to see whether Congress will be willing to, in effect, pass on overarching law which modulates in some way the authorities that it has put in a number of other specific laws. If it's willing to do that, what kind of role is it going to insist on having for itself as part of that process? Don't forget, "itself" is not a thing; it's a collection of committees. When you look at the Congressional veto of individual regulations, it is, in principle, possible for any member of Congress to introduce such a resolution. But in fact, the way most of it's going to happen is to come up out of the committee with oversight over the agency that issues the regulation. Which means the committee that created the agency to start with.

**Ira Millstein**
*Weil, Gotshal and Manges*

The depth of the constitutional problem is demonstrated by Don Rice's point. The rumor is that if the

Congress tacks on a legislative veto to the Regulatory Reform Act, the President will veto the whole Regulatory Reform Act.

## From the Audience:

Mr. Swidler commented about having someone to speak for the center. He mentioned that the politicians' weaknesses were handled by working very closely with the media, which prepared the ground for some difficult decisions. Where have you seen the ground prepared, or where do you have hope it can be, for the center to be spoken for?

## Joseph Swidler
*Leva, Hawes, Symington, Martin and Oppenheimer*

I guess you've put your finger on the heart of the problem. How do you get from here to there? I'm not sure I know. There has never been a time when business's voice was weaker in the legislatures. Business can get some closet support from legislators, who say in private they agree with you. But it's the odd member of Congress who will get up on the floor and put up a fight for an industry position.

This reflects the general decline in the authority of the establishment, government as well as business, and the unwillingness of members of Congress to stick their necks out for business. The general public impression is that business is predatory; the interest of the ordinary citizen is not that of business.

There was a interesting incident in one of the conference committees where a provision was under discussion, and one of the Senators said that he understood there was no use talking about that because he had talked to some interested groups out in the hallway, and they had said they were ready to drop it. So somebody kidded him and said, is that where he got his instructions, out in the hallway, from business interests? Oh, he said, these weren't private businesses; this was a nonprofit group.

177

Well, it is possible for him to listen to them in the hallway, but he wouldn't have listened to a representative of a business organization. This is part of a wave that we're going through now. Business has probably contributed something to it, and the general temper of the times has augmented it.

I'm not sure I agree with the way we've been using the word "partnership." Partner implies a certain quality of relationship between the various groups involved. I don't think the government and business can be partners. The roles are different. But they can work together. They can coordinate. The business interests can understand the objectives of government and of the regulators, and of the legislators they deal with.

Certainly government understands that if they don't cooperate with business, we lose the most productive part of our society. There is no choice in our kind of society but to enable business to operate effectively. And this is becoming harder and harder to do with the low estate in which business now functions.

**From the Audience:**

Most of the questions so far have concerned the adversary role between government and business. Would any of the panel like to discuss the other side of the coin? Specifically, the capture here of regulation, how that would be a barrier against public acceptance of a business-government partnership?

**Harvey Kapnick**
*Arthur Andersen & Co.*

I'm a little reluctant to let the discussion stand at the point at which the last question led us. An awful lot of positive things are happening in Washington. Some of the industrialists here could probably say more about it than I can, but as a disinterested observer I see business beginning to build a relationship in Washington. Business is trying to get the staffs of Congressmen and Senators and other people to understand the whole process better.

Many of the senior business leaders would not want to be out in front. They are more interested in trying the educational route, trying to get facts to the various groups, so that when the decisions *are* made, they are made with as much hard data as possible.

I spend a good deal of my time in Europe; there aren't the same barriers between government and business that there are in this country. When you talk to some of the Germans or some of the Swiss or some of the French or some of the Japanese, they speak of a very in-depth working interest between government and business. It's not unusual for the government in Germany, for example, to help in some way when one of the business organizations is out after a major contract in another country.

It's a matter of getting the process, or the mechanics, to get the job done.

## From the Audience:

It seems to me that there are government programs designed to assist business as well as to control and regulate it. These programs, as well as the regulatory problems, are organized in a fashion to mirror the business structure. I'm curious to know if you agree with that. Are there changes in the organization of business in the United States that would enable the kind of relationship that exists in Germany and France, which you're describing, to come about more easily?

## Harvey Kapnick
*Arthur Andersen & Co.*

There's a whole host of issues in that one. We're a vast nation and we have many different interest groups. It's these various special-issue voter groups or interest groups that tend to create the negative image of business.

The Congress of the United States recognizes that support of business has to be encouraged, as was shown by the tax bill this year. There have to be incentives. More politicians today are realizing, if you talk to them privately, that government probably has failed more than business has failed. They've got to start giving the incentives back to business to try to build these jobs we're talking about.

I see this adversary role, although still very much in the minds of the population of America, as not quite as critical a factor in Washington as it was two or three years ago.

### Ira Millstein
*Weil, Gotshal and Manges*

I would hate to see this wind up in a love feast, because if it did, it would represent a form of government and business which I don't think I'd like. My own feeling is—and I'm an antitrust lawyer by trade—that competition is what made all these companies as good as they are.

The competition between government and business is good. We don't have to hate each other, but goverment is government and business is business. Partnership is a question of getting to know one another's interests and desires a little better. The mechanics I was talking about concern integrating each other in the process so that business can participate in the business of government and government can participate in the business of business.

But if we come to love one another and become part of one another, we won't be the same thing anymore. I think we've got to keep a distance from one another and keep the friction healthy and going. That's what I think will keep the country very, very active. I like healthy skepticism.

### From the Audience:

I was curious about the preliminary results of the Business Round Table study that Arthur Andersen did.

### Harvey Kapnick
*Arthur Andersen and Co.*

I might make two observations. The results are still not final, so I can't talk about them at this point. But I can say, when you start talking about cost, about what can be done, it is a very difficult project. In order to get to the costs, you have to make many subjective judgments. The efforts in human years are very significant on the part of both the companies and anyone who tries to accumulate those numbers. Still you only have a piece of it, because you can't do all of industry; and how do you then extrapolate results into the total?

Once the study is released, it's going to start a debate on the very issue I think is necessary: not whether we need these things, but when you can get them and the degree you can move each year.

# V Toward a New Partnership

Introduction: **Roger B. Smith,**
Executive Vice-President,
General Motors Corporation

Moderator: **Walt W. Rostow,**
Professor of Economics and History,
The University of Texas at Austin

Panelists: **J.J. (Jake) Pickle,**
U.S. House of Representatives,
10th District, Texas

**John Gardner,**
Educator and Statesman

**Charls Walker,**
Lobbyist and Economist;
President,
Charls E. Walker Associates, Inc.

**Frank Ikard,**
President,
American Petroleum Institute;
Partner,
Danzansky, Dickey, Quint
and Gordon

# Summary:
# Toward a New
# Partnership

Early in the conference Douglas Costle mentioned that a partnership between business and government might be considered an "unholy alliance" by some members of the public. At the close of the conference we can see that for most of the panelists, the traditional suspicion among the sectors needs to be tempered with better communication. But the public need not, apparently, fear selfish collusion endangering the public interest.

It is agreed that the emergence of more and more special interest groups has complicated constructive dialogue among different economic sectors of society. If everyone feels his or her own special group is the one victimized by the rest of society, the interaction needed to identify and solve major problems is difficult to achieve. And yet these problems influence everyone's life in America. If any one segment can hold the whole system up for ransom, setting national goals and working out constructive working relationships among traditionally opposing sectors of society becomes nearly impossible.

It seems to many of the panelists that extensive economic education, coupled with a strong middle class, may yet encourage the cooperation of various interest groups. A set of national goals, created in a way that makes every segment of society feel it has participated in the formulation, would help the nation come to grips with its problems, it is suggested. The existence of such goals would, in turn, help shape the attitudes needed for reasoned problem solving.

Throughout the conference an underlying optimism has been felt. The panelists have testified to a belief that business and government are already on the road to a partnership, one that would increase the cooperation necessary to deal successfully with contemporary problems. At the same time, it is recognized that all the assembled power from business and

185

government represented at the symposium is helpless to effect positive change without the support of labor and academia, straight reporting from the press, and a well-educated and involved public.

# V Toward a
# New Partnership

**Roger B. Smith**
*Executive Vice-President,*
General Motors Corporation

*Roger B. Smith graduated from the Graduate Business School at the University of Michigan. He has been with General Motors his entire career, rising in that organization from a general accounting clerk to Executive Vice-President. He is currently responsible for the financial staff of General Motors. In addition, he is in charge of public relations and the relations between industry and government. He is a trustee for the Cranbrook Schools of the Michigan College Foundation. He also serves on the visiting committee of his alma mater, and is a Director of the United Foundation.*

## A New Era of Collaboration

It's a great personal pleasure for me to speak as a businessman on the notion of partnership, or lack of partnership, between American business and American government. The Lyndon Baines Johnson Library, one of the sponsors of this conference, in only a decade has become a significant force in helping to draw together apparently diverse sectors of American society. It has tried to ally them in working together toward the achievement of a better America and a better world. As President Johnson might

187

have said, "We have come to reason together so that we might do what is right."

The cosponsor of this symposium, The University of Texas, represents the American academic community, whose role must be central in the shaping of any government-business partnership. After all, our colleges and universities educate and help mold the future leadership of both business and government. The academic world is also the wellspring of the creative social, political, and industrial policies which determine the kind of world we live in.

The subject of our symposium could hardly be more timely, nor is its achievement more urgent. No major part of the American agenda can be achieved by a single sector of our society working alone. Government alone cannot increase energy supplies, create jobs, safeguard the environment, rebuild the cities, or wipe out discrimination; neither can business; neither can the academic community. Working together, we can.

In many places our interdependence is being translated into action, at long last and to the great benefit of all the American people. We have reason to be encouraged. But there are too many other signs that business and government are not working together as well as they should. The new partnership we speak of today, necessary though it is, emerging though it may be, is still not yet formed.

Witness, for example, how the burden of years of overregulation has sapped America's ability to compete in world trade. Witness the hostility that has so often emerged when legislators and business leaders have differed about the extent and the consequences of this regulation. Witness how many people, highly placed in both government and business, have suspected each other's motives and doubted each other's commitment to the public interest.

### Cooling the Adversarial Relationship

Yes, we still have a way to go in building a more constructive working relationship. A kind of social schizophrenia still darkens a great part of the American mind. I believe that policymaker and profit-maker share a solid foundation of ideals and aspirations for our country, for our children, and for ourselves.

But when a major issue arises, such as how best to fight inflation or how best to add to our energy supply, then we have all too often taken leave of each other. Too frequently the business representative and the government official have stood apart, separate, suspicious, hostile, as adversaries rather than allies.

I add this businessman's voice to all at this symposium who call for a cooling of this adversarial relationship between business and government. Our ideal is partnership. Idealists though we may be, however, we must be practical idealists. We must recognize that this ideal relationship between government and business can never be a partnership in a literal sense.

A government official who is charged to regulate an industry cannot be faithful to his responsibilities if he sees himself, or if others see him, as a partner to that industry. And a corporation executive's primary obligation must always be to the stockholders as well as to society; the extent of the commitment to the pursuit of a particular objective, however commendable, must be judged in this light.

Now there are exceptions, of course. In wartime, for example, business and government must properly be partners in the strictest sense of the term. Apart from national emergencies, the relationship between government and business, to my mind, would be better described as an alliance. We are allied in many common interests; we share many goals; we depend upon each other's cooperation and success. But we are, and we must remain, separate institutions. Each of us is bound by oath or by obligation to

---

"**Business and government . . . are allied in many common interests; we depend upon each other's cooperation and success. But we are, and we must remain, separate institutions. Each of us is bound by oath or obligation to those we represent. Nevertheless, the word 'partnership' has meaning here, representing a kind of positive working relationship . . . .**"

those we represent. Nevertheless, the word "partnership" has meaning here, representing a kind of positive working relationship in the broader interests of both stockholders and citizens.

Nowhere are these shared interests more entwined than in the well-being of our economy. In today's fiercely competitive world, business and government can no longer afford to be adversaries, for what is essentially at stake is America's place in the world and the maintenance and expansion of our people's standard of living.

To achieve this closer harmony, I as a business leader recommend that the first thing business must do is recognize that it can never return to the laissez faire capitalism of another time. Understandably, we may long for a return to simpler days, to the uncomplicated world of buy-and-sell that our predecessors knew. But the clock of history does not turn back. The government's involvement in business is a fact of life and, in appropriate amounts, it is necessary. In some cases, it is even to be sought.

### Business's Approach to Government

Business people must approach their relationship with government with reason and tact. They must appreciate the policymaker's obligation to the interests of the entire public. When business people feel their interests, or those of their customers, owners, or employees, are being damaged by ill-considered legislation or by short-sighted government policy, they should approach Congress and the regulatory bodies with specific constructive proposals.

People in business must speak against what they think is unreasonable and wrong; they should also propose a course which they believe would be reasonable and right. Never should they resort to partisan arguments, nor should they question the integrity of government officials.

We in business need to present more facts and more figures and less rhetoric and less finger-pointing. Every argument and proposal we take to Washington or advance in our speeches should place fair emphasis on the factual, scientific, and legal merits of our position.

Business can also improve its relationship with the government by getting its own house in order. Many, in fact a great many, of the regulations that burden business today need not be on the books at all. They might not be if we in business had done earlier what we are doing today.

By doing well what we do best, by serving and satisfying our customers, we could have avoided much of today's economic regulation. I can say that at least in General Motors we acknowledge the antecedent of regulation to be our old shortcomings in satisfying our customers.

## Government's Attitude toward Business

Those are some of the things business people can do. But government people must also contribute to the building of our new partnership. Government people might begin by altering their attitudes toward business, and particularly toward business profits.

Almost every criticism of business carries the implication that business people are motivated solely by lust for profit: not a reasonable profit, but an enormous profit, an unconscionable profit; and that business will stop at nothing to get it. This attitude is wrong, as wrong as the views that all in government place their personal interests before the public interest.

Today in our country businesses do not reap exorbitant profits. Last year America's manufacturing corporations earned an average profit of only 5.3 percent of sales. That's about a nickel for each dollar of sales. Furthermore, the ultimate beneficiaries of these profits are the people and the country, for profits have built our country just as surely as they have built General Motors.

Profits have provided jobs, financed hospitals and schools, paid for police and fire departments, for libraries,

---

"We in business need to present more facts and more figures and less rhetoric and less finger-pointing. Every argument and proposal we take to Washington or advance in our speeches should place fair emphasis on the factual, scientific, and legal merits of our position."

for our national defense system—indeed for our entire national life. Profit should not be a dirty word in the capitals of our nation.

If government were to recognize that business must prosper if America is to hold its place in the world, this recognition alone would do much to ease the tensions between us. More than just acknowledging this necessity for profits, I think government should in fact encourage it. Government could promote the economic well-being so vital to all of us, and hold down inflation, by adhering to sound monetary and fiscal policies. It could also develop a tax program which would encourage business to invest in economic growth and provide for the creation of jobs.

Government should do what it can to promote a better business climate to give American business the profit incentive it needs to be more innovative and more competitive in our shrinking world. Government should do this, not for the sake of business, but for the sake of the people the government represents.

Believe me, the challenge of world-wide competition is a promise. Like it or not, America and American business are in direct and intense competition with all other nations of the world like we have never been before. We compete not only for customers in the marketplace, but also for influence in the world. To compete aggressively for either, we must have a closer alliance between business and government. It is, remember, an alliance that all other industrial democracies in the world already enjoy.

Government could further promote a better relationship with business by remembering that financial resources are just as finite as natural resources. Government lives by a budget and so must business. Excessive regulatory measures

---

**"Government should do what it can to promote a better business climate to give American business the profit incentive it needs to be more innovative and more competitive in our shrinking world. Government should do this, not for the sake of business, but for the sake of the people the government represents."**

which impose cost upon the consumer without commensurate benefit serve no one's best interest. They are purely and simply waste, and it is a waste that not even our country can long afford.

Finally, to the fullest extent possible, government should let business carry its own share of the partnership. It should rely more on a free market system and less on central planning. Central planning is tremendously difficult. In no society has it ever worked well, or for long. In contrast, free market economy responds easily on a daily basis to the natural interaction of supply and demand. Its great beauty is that it plans for itself.

All of us, but especially those in government, should be more appreciative of this marvelous mechanism, and we should let it function for all of us. We should certainly be sure of what we're doing before we try to replace it with anything else.

## The New Generation of Business People

I believe this new partnership will emerge, and here's why: A new generation of business people is coming into the leadership of American companies and corporations. Now, in many ways, they are like the generation that they are succeeding. They have read their Adam Smith, and they know the necessity of profit for themselves, as well as for our free society.

But I suggest that the members of this new generation differ in several important ways from their predecessors. In the first place, they have never known a time when government was not deeply involved in the private affairs of business.

They began their careers after the Depression, after the New Deal, after World War II, and after the early battles over government regulation had already been fought. They still adhere, as I so staunchly do, to the old value of economic freedom, free markets, and free choices.

But they are much quicker to acknowledge the complexity of our time. They are more ready to admit the need for some degree of government regulation. In fact, John

DeButts, before his retirement from AT&T, said he had come to the belief that today every aspiring chief executive officer in business should be required to spend at least one year in Washington. This, he said, would better enable a young business executive to distinguish between shadow and substance in the company's relationship with the government.

There are exceptions, of course, but at least a decade has separated the time when this new generation of Americans came to the leadership of government and when it rose to the top of business. That separation in time may account for much of the friction that came into the business-government relationships in the decades of the sixties and has endured right into the seventies.

Remember President Kennedy's inaugural: "Now the torch has passed to a new generation of Americans"? And at least something of that idealism and widened view of the world which characterized President Kennedy's New Frontier and President Johnson's Great Society are now lighting the minds of the business leaders of today. These leaders are now in a position to ally the interests of business and the interests of government.

Together now we must dedicate ourselves to the healing of the hostilities which have grown in the intervening years. We must recognize that the most committed champion of the consumer today is the business leader who depends upon the customer's favor for his livelihood. We must ask ourselves in fairness, "Does an adversary relationship still serve the public interest, or is much of it like the Cold War: better to be remembered as a necessity only in its time?"

Many of the calls we hear today for ever more stringent regulation of business are really a throwback to another

---

**"At least something of that idealism and widened view of the world which characterized President Kennedy's New Frontier and President Johnson's Great Society are now lighting the minds of the business leaders of today. These leaders are now in a position to ally the interests of business and the interests of government."**

decade. Much of business's railing against regulation is actually an echo of a distant debate. Now is the time for reason. A time begin to put to rest even an empty argument. It troubles us still, but it can best be settled by those who see both the necessity and the advantage of the closest cooperation between the business of our nation and our nation's business.

I submit that the new generation of business leaders still wants success in business terms. But it also wants to work with government in influencing policy, in choosing the course that our nation will take. Those in business perceive this as one of the new tasks of the corporate citizen: they know it can only be accomplished hand-in-hand with government.

With its heightened awareness of world affairs, the new generation has come to understand, much more than its predecessors, that business must take on far greater responsibilities in a modern society. It must continue to compete in the traditional marketplace where goods and services are sold, but it also must enter a new marketplace: a marketplace of ideas where the forces that shape are society are determined.

So in these ways the new business leaders are different from all who have gone before. Their careers were molded into new shapes by the rush of history and events after the war. As their careers were changed, so were their minds changed. They experienced an evolution of attitudes about business and about its place in the world. This new way of thinking is a key asset for survival in today's complex business environment. But more importantly, the new era

---

"With its heightened awareness of world affairs, the new generation has come to understand, much more than its predecessors, that business must take on far greater responsibilities in a modern society. It must continue to compete in the traditional marketplace where goods and services are sold, but it also must enter a new marketplace: a marketplace of ideas where the forces that shape our society are determined."

has brought business leaders closer in their thinking to the leaders of government and perhaps the leaders of government are also altering their thinking concerning business.

## What's at Stake

I can speak from personal experience and observation about the evolution of attitudes in the new generation of business leadership, but as far as government is concerned, I can only express the hope that a similar evolution of attitude is taking place. Indeed, it must.

There is an urgency here which we would be foolish to ignore. At stake is nothing less than our survival among other nations. Our world has been getting smaller and smaller all the time. The nations of the world today are connected and competing as never before. But as I have said, there is mounting evidence that the suspicion and distrust are giving way to sanity and stability, particularly in the relationship between business and government.

This nation of ours is great. It was born with a promise of greatness, and it has yet to achieve its full potential. With our public and our private sectors working more constructively together, in an alliance, if not in a strict partnership, the day when that full potential will be realized may be fast approaching.

*The basically opposing perspectives of business and government are apparent in this final discussion. The participants include a pure politician in Jake Pickle and a pure corporate executive in Roger Smith, plus others who have held a variety of roles in long and productive careers.*

*The primary objective of business, what colors most business decisions, is how to compete in providing goods and services to the needs or*

---

**"There is an urgency here which we would be foolish to ignore. At stake is nothing less than our survival among other nations."**

*demands of the market and at the same time make enough profit to survive. Government, on the other hand, to serve the people, must think in terms of equal employment rights, social security benefit provisions, pollution problems, and so forth.*

*Government also steps in with regulatory action concerning safety rules, health care, and so on. Many of the panelists see business itself doing these tasks to a greater and greater extent today, out of simple self-interest.*

*The primary objectives of business and government differ, although both sectors depend on a healthy economy and mutually support means to that end. The last panel, in looking toward the future for a business-government partnership, discusses how both productivity and equity can be maintained in the face of the vast array of special interest or pressure groups described by John Gardner. Education and increased economic understanding are suggested as possible means.*

*But the panel frankly puzzles over the question of how to forge new institutions compatible with American beliefs in a time of shrinking resources and increased international competition.*

**J.J. (Jake) Pickle**
*Congressman,*
10th District,
State of Texas

*Jake Pickle began public life in the National Youth Administration, serving as Area Director from 1938 to 1941. He has been the representative of the 10th District of Texas from the 88th to the 96th Congresses. He is the Chairman of the Subcommittee on Social Security of the House Ways and Means Committee and a member of the committee looking at unemployment insurance. He is an expert on transport and health care, science, and management-labor relations, and is an ardent defender and promoter of the 10th District of Texas. He is a national expert—as only an experienced Congressman can become—for he has lived with national problems over longer periods of time than have members of the Executive Branch of government.*

## Toward a New Partnership

There seems to be a good bit of suspicion going on between government and business. I experienced much the same attitude years ago when I was a member of the State Democratic Executive Committee. People would say: "Do you know Jake Pickle?" and the answer would be: "No, but I suspect him."

Though there's a lot of suspicion, you'll find at least ninety-eight percent of those men and women in government are good, honorable, hard-working people. You get about what you deserve, maybe a little better in most instances. What we've got to do is get a better understanding of what we're both trying to do.

I hope we can have an accommodation between business and government. I'm a little bit defensive because I have the feeling you're talking about government—me, the elected official—when what you're really talking about is the bureaucracy. You see, I have as much trouble with the bureaucracy as you business people do. I have more, because every time you've got a complaint you bring it to me to go to the bureaucracy. I spend about fifty to seventy-five percent of my time being a referee between the business community and the government bureaucracy.

## Government as Referee

The government is not just a spectator in this process. We are the referees. Because sooner or later nearly all these controversies you talk about come across our desks. We have to make a decision about what is right for business and what is best for the individual. I wish it weren't that simple, but I think it is.

Why is government like that? We're so involved because, one, we spend a lot of federal money. You business people like that federal money to spend. You like it in billions. As long as we have that kind of money we're going to be involved through the tax code, through grants, through loans, or combinations of these. Two, profit today, perhaps unfortunately, is largely determined by how well your CPA can handle the tax code. You either make a profit or you don't, depending on how you can wriggle the tax code to your advantage.

We could stop all that if you business people wanted to. We could stop it by just having a flat rate: reduce your corporate tax from the forty-eight percent Charley Walker would say is too high down to the twenty percent and do

---

"I have as much trouble with the bureaucracy as you business people do. I have more, because every time you've got a complaint you bring it to me to go to the bureaucracy. I spend about fifty to seventy-five percent of my time being a referee between the business community and the government bureaucracy."

away with all the deductions and exemptions. We haven't done that, and I doubt if we will. The reason is, you business people do not want a flat tax rate. You have learned how to make a profit using the tax code. You have learned how to take advantage of it, as you should.

A flat tax rate would cause an outcry from institutions such as The University of Texas; charitable and educational institutions would say: "We cannot operate if you do away with all tax deductions." The government is involved.

I've noticed over the years that when times are good, the economy is booming, your sales are up, the average businessman says to me: "Just keep out of our business. We're doing all right. The less government, the better."

But you let a recession come in, you let unemployment get a little higher, and I am grabbed by the arm, literally, almost threateningly, and told, "What in the hell are you fellows going to do about the economy? You've got it so screwed up, you've got to do something. What are you going to do?"

**Problems with Government**

Now, we can't do both. But we're called on to do a lot of things in this day and time we must do. I would make two or three admissions: one, there's too much paperwork. It is one of the tragedies of our time that any person in business, particularly in a small business, must devote some twenty percent of expenditures to just filling out forms of one kind or another. Somehow we've got to do better.

Two, we've got too many rules and regulations, I'll admit. Most of the people in the bureaus are good people. They're people who have been selected from the 10th District, from New York, from Chicago, from California— just average American individuals who are doing the best they can. But we've got to carry out the laws we have passed.

---

"I've noticed over the years that when times are good, the economy is booming, your sales are up, the average businessman says to me: 'Just keep out of our business. We're doing all right. The less government, the better.'"

We've got too many people in the bureaus who want to do it too well. We could use a little more common sense; we could cure a great many of the problems we've got. We're doing better in this respect, but there's sure a lot of improvement needed ahead.

## The Influence of Business

You know why we have all these rules and regulations? Because business people want them. I've watched the process over the years. Every time some bill comes up, whether it affects the environment or just affects business generally, the average group comes to Washington representing some business organization. They insist on having this amendment and that amendment.

You see, business does not trust the government; business does not trust the bureaucracy. As a result, we have produced great numbers of rules and regulations, so as not to be imposed on. Now they're on the books, and I don't know what we're going to do about it.

I want to keep the free enterprise system. It must be maintained. Overall, we're going well in this country, and I don't think we ought to despair. I think we're doing better than any nation on the face of the globe. It's good to have an introspective look, but I want to throw out another point: there are two doctrines which have dominated the United States goverment's economic policies for the last thirty years.

One is Keynesian; that is, "Spend your way to better living," which produces either accelerating inflation of wages or price controls.

The other is monetarism; that is, you beat inflation by reducing the money supply growth rate, which works a great hardship on those who can least bear it.

---

**"But you let a recession come in, you let unemployment get a little higher, and I am grabbed by the arm, literally, almost threateningly, and told, 'What in the hell are you fellows going to do about the economy? You've got it so screwed up, you've got to do something. What are you going to do?'"**

Neither of these doctrines addresses the issue of great importance: How do we create both a stable and an increasingly productive economy? After all, rising productivity is the only way a society can provide for more and more people.

## Innovations and Incentives

What is the solution? Economic stability *and* growth depend on innovation, the process of providing new and better products and services.

Like anything else, innovations are not going to be forthcoming without adequate incentives. Right now incentives are not adequate. Here's why: since World War II more and more groups have learned to use government as a shield from competition and shift in demand. Having eliminated or at least minimized the challenge of changed circumstances, their incentive to search for better ways of serving other people just hasn't been there.

What we've got is not a shortage of capital but a shortage of risk-taking. By risk-taking I mean the process of transforming an internal competitive threat into an external challenge for developing successful innovation. We've still got to stress capital formation; but we've got capital around.

We're getting to the point in American government where we've got to consider how we can somehow protect the little person in business. There are too many big corporations buying out and writing off small businesses for tax purposes. This practice hurts productivity, and is a very serious problem in this country.

---

"**What is the solution?** Economic stability *and* **growth depend on innovation, the process of providing new and better products and services. Like anything else, innovations are not going to be forthcoming without adequate incentives.**"

**John Gardner**
*Educator and Statesman*

*John Gardner's career spans both the public and the private
sectors. At the moment he is engaged in examining the
problems of private foundations, including universities—
those groups hard pressed by inflation and other contemporary realities. He was Secretary of Health, Education and
Welfare from 1965 to 1968. He has a Ph.D. in psychology and
has taught in that field. He was President of the Carnegie
Corporation, and a leader in education in the 1950s and
1960s. He directed Common Cause between 1970 and 1977.
He is also on the Board of Directors of Shell Oil Company,
New York Telephone, American Airlines, and Time, Inc.*

I don't see two great groups trying somehow to
overcome their offensiveness to one another and get
together.

The Executive Branch, one of these great groups, is not
an entity. It is a collection of fragments, each of which has an
enduring partnership with some part of the private sector.
That's one of the problems.

### The Growth of Special Interests

Very few people recognize that since World War II there
has been an enormous proliferation of special-interest
groups—highly organized, effective political forces. If you
ask the citizen in the street about special interests, he or she is
likely to say, "Well, there's business and there's labor," and
maybe add "farmers." The average citizen has no inkling of
the extraordinary growth of organizations.

First of all, business itself is not a single group. It's thousands of groups, often at odds with one another.

Labor involves various powerful groups, often disagreeing with one another. Then there are the maritime groups, the agribusiness groups, the major professions and subprofessions; religious groups, racial groups, regional groups; powerful states with strong lobbies in Washington; institutional groups such as hospitals and junior colleges. Not every such group, but almost all of them, are now highly organized for advancing their own interests.

Each is at work linking into its own little piece of the federal government.

It is entirely in accord with our pluralism that all of these groups pursue their special interest as vigorously and forcefully as they can. That's their constitutional right, and it's part of our system. As long as it's done openly, as long as the interest groups do not use money in ways that corrupt the public process, and as long as people who are pursuing what they conceive to be the public interest also get a chance to speak. Everyone differs on what the public interest is.

When you're dealing with a cluster of problems such as energy or inflation or the cities, where there's a basketful of problems rather than a single problem, the groups are so numerous and so tenacious as to paralyze the policymaking process.

How many times have we seen a major American city facing the gravest possible municipal problems paralyzed by the functioning of special forces? Each special group has achieved a partial veto power. Nobody has the power to solve the problem.

---

"It is entirely in accord with our pluralism that all of these groups pursue their special interest as vigorously and forcefully as they can.... As long as it's done openly, as long as the interest groups do not use money in ways that corrupt the public process, and as long as people who are pursuing what they conceive to be the public interest also get a chance to speak. Everyone differs on what the public interest is."

In an oddly self-destructive way the parts are warring against the whole. This is not a political dilemma. It is the central problem of pluralism today. We're moving rapidly toward a society so intricately organized and interlocked that the working of the whole system may be halted if one of the parts stops functioning. Any part can hold the whole system up for ransom, as the air-traffic controllers and many other groups have discovered, to their delight.

Thus the problem becomes: How do you rise above the paralyzing effect of all these partnerships, each tenaciously pursuing its own special interest, and face up to the larger interests we all share?

How do you get each of the organized groups, whether it's business or labor or the professions, to realize that they are subsystems of a larger system which is society, and if the larger system fails, the subsystems can't survive?

---

"In an oddly self-destructive way the parts are warring against the whole. This is ... the central problem of pluralism today.... Any part can hold the whole system up for ransom."

**Charls Walker**
*Charls E. Walker
Associates, Inc.*

*Since 1973, Charls Walker has headed Charls E. Walker
Associates, Inc., which combines lobbying with economic
consulting in the area of business-government relations. He
has been a professor of finance at the Wharton School of
Business (1948-1950) and at The University of Texas at
Austin (1950-1954). He has served as an economist for two
Federal Reserve Banks, Philadelphia and Dallas, and has
also worked with the Republic National Bank in Dallas. Dr.
Walker served as assistant to Secretary Robert Anderson in
the Treasury from 1959 to 1961. He reached the rank of
Deputy in 1972 while serving in the Treasury Department.*

I've got to say a word about Jake. He's not only a pure
politician, as you found out, but he is *not* an economist.
There's a lot of talk about Keynesianism being dead. If it
wasn't already, Jake drove the last nail in the coffin just a
while ago.

But he's a very astute politician, as I found out last night.
Midway in our five-hour stop on the apron at Dulles Airport
in the Pickle Special, he stood up for all to hear and said:
"Henceforth this airplane will be known as the Henry
Gonzales Special."

Concerning the need for partnership, or a positive
working relationship between business and government,
what you're talking about depends on how you might view
participatory democracy.

**Participatory Democracy**

What do we mean by participatory democracy? I went

to Webster, who defines participatory democracy as "providing opportunity for individual participation." That doesn't tell us much. Going to the voting booth gives you the opportunity for individual participation. So I went to William Safire's great book, *The Political Dictionary* (Random House, 1978), and found two definitions. One, "Citizen involvement in the affairs that affect him." The second definition was even more intriguing: "Leadership rejection"; meaning, I guess, that the people have to get in and take leadership.

This whole conference seems to be an exercise in participatory democracy. The leadership rejection Safire refers to, and the importance of the positive relationship between business and government referred to earlier in the conference, are both obviously vital concerns.

In some areas the adversary process must continue; in contrast, there's one area a true partnership is needed. We very badly need a 1980s model of the Reconstruction Finance Corporation, run by a 1980s model Jesse Jones. In contrast to what you might think a business representative such as myself would think of the Reconstruction Finance Corporation concept, I think it's as American as—well, as "Kosher Burritos."

Such a public-private partnership as the Reconstruction Finance Corporation is needed to do things that the private enterprise system finds very difficult to do for itself. We wouldn't have had the railroads, we wouldn't have had the canals, we wouldn't have had many of the things that made this country prosperous and great if it hadn't been for a

---

"In some areas the adversary process must continue; in contrast, there's one area a true partnership is needed. We very badly need a 1980s model of the Reconstruction Finance Corporation, run by a 1980s model Jesse Jones. In contrast to what you might think a business representative such as myself would think of the Reconstruction Finance Corporation concept, I think it's as American as—well, as 'Kosher Burritos.'"

public-private operation doing things that private enterprise alone cannot do because of the expense, the risk, or what-have-you.

### Outline for Partnership

We need, in summary, a Reconstruction Finance Corporation with about four windows: one to provide freight transportation, rebuilding our railroads in particular, which are in very bad shape; one to deal with high technology areas that are very expensive, such as supersonic transport—whether or not you are for it, it's the sort of thing that can be done only through a public-private partnership; one to provide for commercializing processes that can't be done without such a partnership, such as in the energy area; and, finally, one window to handle the problems of the cities. I'd make certain that the person who ran this Reconstruction Finance Corporation was a pretty hard-nosed operator.

How do we get from where we are to this positive working relationship? We are already on the road to partnership. We saw convincing signs of it in the 95th Congress, which may well go down in history as the Congress which started the pendulum moving back from governmental and regulatory approaches to problems to market solutions to problems.

Item: the defeat of the Consumer Protection Agency. Whether you were for or against this decision, many people spoke up and said, "We don't need that type of help, not to that extent."

Item: the defeat of certain labor legislation having to do with common situs picketing and labor law revision.

Even more important, the rejection of an energy bill which relied upon government regulation as opposed to the market system and incentives to produce more.

And finally, that remarkable tax bill which reversed the trend of several decades and reduced taxes on the middle class, reduced taxes on capital formation—on those items so important to productivity and growth.

### Newly Ascendent Middle Class

Part of this trend was due to the influence and increased

Charls Walker
Charls E. Walker Associates, Inc.

involvement, as Roger Smith was talking about earlier, of businessmen and the business community. But there's more to it than that. We can now discern in this country a newly ascendent political group with clout.

Big labor had most of the clout from the 1930s until recently. Labor took it from big business, who had it before. But now the middle class is in the driver's seat. The middle class, defined in its own image, not as statisticians define it, but as a family with an income of about fifteen to fifty thousand dollars a year. These are the people who are more important in electing the members of Congress than anyone else. And Congress, in turn, as a democratic institution, is reflecting the desires of the middle class.

Some "for instances" to illustrate why we're already down the road on this constructive partnership, to wind up:

Legislation, not perfect, but positive, was passed in the last Congress to work out the problems of the Arab boycott of American goods so we could have a balanced trading relationship in the Middle East. The basic thrust of the legislation was developed by a group of businessmen working with Jewish organizations.

Item: there will be debates in welfare legislation in this Congress ahead; again the business community is working with key legislators to examine alternative solutions to the welfare problem.

Item: in Jake Pickle's own field, social security, various proposals are coming in from the business community to deal with problems. Closely tied to social security is Senator Long's proposal for a significant change in the tax structure, a proposal to substitute a value-added tax for parts of other taxes, including social security. A good idea or a bad idea? It needs to be examined, and it is, constructively.

Item: with respect to the needed growth in productivity Jake referred to, the business community is working actively with members of the tax-writing and related committees in Congress. First to help produce better tax legislation, legislation that will promote productivity. Second, to aid the round-table study of ways to increase productivity through changes in the regulatory process. Arthur Andersen is releasing the study shortly.

The business community is working actively in the area of spending control, avoiding the danger of a strict constitutional amendment approach while building ways to control spending, so we can finally get on top of inflation.

My thesis is we don't have to make a U-turn in the road. We don't even have to make a ninety-degree turn in the road. Over the past several years, particularly in the last two or three years, we have been moving ahead in a constructive, positive relationship between business and government. With the uncommon good sense and monumental political clout of the middle class, coupled with a new generation of business leadership Roger Smith referred to, I think we can get there from here.

**Frank Ikard**
*President,*
American Petroleum Institute

*From 1963 to 1979 Frank Ikard has been the President and Chief Executive Officer of the American Petroleum Institute, which acquired under his leadership a reputation for generating accurate and valuable statistics permitting the study and analysis of the petroleum situation. He is a lawyer in the firm of Danzansky, Dickey, Tydings, Quint and Gordon. For ten years, 1951-1961, he was a member of the U.S. Congress. A 1936 law graduate of The University of Texas at Austin, he has served on The University of Texas System Board of Regents. He was a member of the American delegation to the United Nations Conference on the Human Environment. He has served on the advisory board of Georgetown University's Center for Strategic Studies in Washington and also on the boards of several industrial and financial institutions.*

## The Fragmentation of Society

Let's return to the central question John Gardner so eloquently touched on—the fragmentation of society. Fragmentation involves giving to one relatively small minority the capability of vetoing programs, and of hindering the movement of the whole society.

We have seen the destruction, although we won't admit it, of the national political parties. There is neither a Democratic nor a Republican Party in this country that has any responsibility in the national sense. We've seen fragmentation and special-issue and special-interest approaches where people seem to zero in on one question and have no concern about all the others.

We've seen that approach lead to a sterile situation that has dried up broadly based people's interest in the government process—people like John Gardner who have been, and would be again, great public servants, willing to spend their time in public service, particularly in the Executive Branch.

There are a few pure politicians, like Jake Pickle, who still want to run for office. But I'm talking about those people who aren't politicians who could make a real contribution. It's extremely difficult to get people to accept responsible positions on the executive side; fragmentation is the reason for it. If we're going to have a meaningful partnership we're going to have to communicate better with each other and to be more tolerant of each other's views.

**Regulation**

As business people we have to understand that regulation, as onerous as it is and as bad as we find the times when we have to live under it, has been brought about by a real or perceived need. Regulation doesn't just walk in off the street. We have regulation because someone in the legislature saw a need for it. What we have to deal with is largely a communications problem.

I share Mr. Smith's sensitivity about central planning. It's imperative we develop a means of establishing national goals whereby every segment of society can participate. A monumental example of a failure to do that is our current energy situation. We have absolutely refused, as a nation, to come to grips with probably the most important question, in an economic sense, that faces us.

It's not new; it's been going on for at least ten years. There is not a person in this room who can tell me with any

---

"It's imperative we develop a means of establishing national goals whereby every segment of society can participate. A monumental example of a failure to do that is our current energy situation. We have absolutely refused, as a nation, to come to grips with probably the most important question, in an economic sense, that faces us."

certainty what our national energy policy is. Yet this audience has a far greater capacity to understand than any other you could assemble in this community. Now that's a sad commentary. We cannot have a partnership in anything unless we know where we're going. First we have to get together, not only in the area of energy, but nationally.

On the energy side, we have created a hodgepodge of regulation that has diminished supply. We are in fact today, as we sit here with existing policy, subsidizing the Organization of Petroleum Exporting Countries. Rather interesting, if it weren't so tragic.

We must devise some means of collectively agreeing on national goals. Once we have established those goals, or directions, from a national standpoint, the private sector should be given the responsibility of trying to reach those goals.

*The Moderator asks John Gardner: To what extent would the emergence of a consensus about national priorities make the pressure of special-interest groups more manageable?*

**John Gardner**
*Educator and Statesman*

A consensus about priorities would have an enormous effect. Getting from here to there is a huge problem. Not only the complexity of things such as the energy problem and inflation, but an attitudinal difficulty, just has me baffled.

Everybody feels like a victim today. This is the era of the victim.

I was talking to a friend of mine in business the other day who said, "We feel like we're huddled in a bomb shelter."

Well, go over to Sixteenth Street in Washington to the AFL-CIO headquarters. They feel like the country has never been so antilabor, that they're harassed, persecuted, and so forth.

Go to the American Medical Association in Chicago, go to the National Education Association, the Pentagon, wherever. Everyone has this feeling of being besieged. Their little group is somehow being ill-treated, ill-used, by the rest of society. I haven't begun to name all the groups that feel that way. If you feel like a victim, it's pretty hard to engage in constructive interaction.

I don't know how you get over that. It's a curious product of our fragmentation. But it is as real an element as anything we've talked about.

### Charls Walker
*Charls E. Walker Associates, Inc.*

Let me tell a Texas good news/bad news story.

This has to do with the wheeler-dealer firm up in Dallas that was buying up property all over the place. They saw something they coveted down in Houston. They sent down their best negotiator and said: "You can bid up to thirty million dollars for this."

He called back in a couple of days, and said: "Chief, I've got some good news and some bad news."

The chief said, "What's the good news?"

"We can get this for $28 million, saving two million."

The chief said, "That's great. What's the bad news?"

He said, "These cowboys want $750 cash down for earnest money."

That's a true story.

### Special Interest Groups

The bad news is the point that John Gardner made about all these special groups. It's not new. The suffragettes, the prohibition people, this and that—we've had special interest groups for a long time. We haven't had as many, and they haven't been nearly so effective, and I guess their communication system and a lot of other things weren't as big. But my impression is that most people, like the people in the middle class I've been talking about, are *not* members of these groups.

And many people *do* feel ripped off. They feel ripped off by big business, they feel ripped off by big labor, and they feel ripped off by big government. And when it comes to the last of those three, in relation to our number-one problem now, inflation, this is where the people feel ripped off the most. We've got to get inflation under control even to have a chance of moving toward constructive partnership.

You see how the people feel ripped off in their demands for control of government spending; you see the same feeling beind Proposition 13; you see it in many, many ways. They are speaking out, loudly. A preeminent issue now coming up from the people is whether we should have a constitutional amendment to balance the budget every year, or a constitutional convention designed to produce an amendment to balance the budget every year.

That happens to be a very bad idea. But it's bad news/good news, in the sense that it will lead to the type of disciplining in and within the Congress we need. Congress will have to bring spending under control. The people have had a bellyfull, and for the first time in many years when it comes to government spending, deficit financing, too much money creation, and inflation, good politics and good economics are going along together.

A fundamental reason for my optimism in general, and the reason I don't get so uptight about special-interest groups, is that I have great confidence in the good sense of the middle class. It has to be your most stable political group. You saw what happened in Germany when inflation wiped out the middle class in the 1920s. It's a compassionate group, a well-educated group, and I'm happy to be in their hands.

**Frank Ikard**
*American Petroleum Institute*

I think Charley Walker spoke very eloquently about his special-interest group.

This is precisely what we're talking about; we've had special-interest groups all through our history. But I don't think we ever had a time when they broke down the central organizations that gave direction, in a political sense, to this country, as they're doing now.

We're on the verge of becoming, or already have become, a country of minority rule. Not minority rule in the usual social sense that we use the word "minority," but in the true sense that fewer than a majority of the people vote for the candidate elected. I would be surprised if any opposed candidate got fifty percent of the vote last November in a national election —if any did, it was a very few.

What that says to us is that our society is so politically fragmented, so turned off by the whole system, that people are simply *not* participating. We have to communicate, and get people back involved before we can even think about partnership.

### John Gardner
*Educator and Statesman*

Maybe I can salvage a good word, participation, by picking up on that point about the various organized groups threatening any central means of resolving fragmentation. In the 1960s citizen participation meant a kind of impulsive, spontaneous getting together: citizens meeting to talk about their concerns and worries. I sat through an awful lot of those meetings because I had to; I was working on the cities. The seats were hard and the halls were drafty, and the citizens were long-winded.

I had a lot of time to think, and one of the things that really struck me was that the process going on in that hall was not connected to any central nervous system, so to speak. The meeting ended and it kind of blew over, and nothing happened.

And down the street ten blocks away was city hall or some miles away was the state capitol or the office of your Congressman. All of these elements were set up as part of a network, a nervous system, set up a couple of hundred years ago, presumably to be instruments of citizen participation. And if that's not what it is, I don't know what it is.

When I think of citizen participation I think of a form
that recognizes the primacy of our institutions or represen-
tation. I'm going to raise hell, but finally I'm going to leave
things in Jake Pickle's hands. I want to leave things to him
and his colleagues to fight out.

I want to work through that system. I don't see any other
way than to finally put it in the hands of somebody who is
going to make the trade-offs and deal with the situations in
which equally worthy groups want mutually incompatible
things. Unless you want to shoot it out you turn to the much
maligned arena of politics.

**Jake Pickle**
*Congressman*

Before I respond to Mr. Gardner, I want to thank
Charley Walker for not classifying me as an economist. We
have had those fellows parade before our Ways and Means
Committee end on end, and they never reach a conclusion.

You talk about people feeling like they're victims—I can
understand that. None of you have said the victim is the
person who sits in the Congressional seat and has to vote!

The Congress has to listen to not one, but hundreds of
various groups. In the last ten to fifteen years many of them
have formed, and they have decided that they can affect our
democracy—that they can make a difference. They're good
groups, they're sincere, and they come at us with all these
facts and information. Well, obviously, when we listen and
we make a vote, we vote yes or no. We can't vote "maybe," or
"if" or "perhaps." We've got to put it one way.

Now, when we do that, as we must do, whether we're
right or wrong, a lot of these people are going to be
disillusioned because their side has not won. The danger is
that if, as that happens, they feel their voice doesn't make any
difference, that hurts democracy. But I'm not alarmed about
it, because this has been going on since the Republic was
founded, and it's going to keep on. That's just democracy.
The system works after all.

## Roger Smith
*General Motors Corporation*

I didn't think when I sat down here I would be coming to the defense of Congressman Pickle. First of all, he doesn't need it.

There are some bad regulations on our books; they are on there for two reasons. First, in a lot of the things we as a nation want to set up goals for, we lack hard, scientific evidence to help us know what it is we're trying to do.

We all want clean air, but I don't think I've ever found a definition of what clean air is, with all my experience with the problem. We get evidence here, there, everywhere, depending on what the particular group offering it is driving at.

A second reason for some of the bad regulations is that the interest groups that get behind an issue have a typical American way of doing things.

People in interest groups decide if they want four of something they'd better go ask for eight, because they're probably only going to get three. Put that attitude with the fact that you don't have good scientific data and you put tremendous pressure on a Congressman.

What happens is a little bell rings in his office and he has to go vote on something. He's voting on a set of standards; like he says, he doesn't get even a broad range. Sometimes three hard numbers are put into law, like they were on the automobile emission standards. The scientific world of the United States, particularly, and foreign experts too, say they probably are not the right three numbers.

But Congressman Pickle didn't get a chance to vote on what he thought the right numbers were. He's got to vote yes or no on a set of numbers. Once something has been decided on we shouldn't decide it's perfect and stop. We should go back and check: "Hey, did we really do the right thing here? Has this turned out the way we wanted it to? Or, now that we know better, should we go back and redo it?"

The major thing that prevents this happening now is the tremendous work load the agencies and the Congress are under. They seem so busy getting out new regulations they hardly have time to go back and fix the old ones.

What we need in Washington, not just for business but for the country, is sober reappraisal of the regulations we already have, not the forthcoming ones. We need to stop and see if we have in fact done what is best for the country. Maybe, somehow, we can get a mechanism to do that. I don't quite know how.

I've seen all the regulatory council coming out, but they're only looking down the road. I don't know what mechanism is set up to review the past ones. It's up to Congressman Pickle and the elected representatives to do that job.

## Jake Pickle
*Congressman*

When we talk about what government does, it sounds like government is trying to run your businesses. Or that government, through this power of the printing press, is trying to determine how the economy goes. I don't think the government is trying to do that, or that we ought to do that.

We should be limited in what we do. Business has relied on the steadying hand of the federal government to stabilize the free enterprise system. They have done that. But we, as government, are not trying to solve all the problems.

The free enterprise system, business, is the employer of the first resort, which is as it should be, rather than government the employer of the last resort. We're not trying to run the economy. We can't spend enough money to do it.

The answer is found in how we get business going. Again, I'm concerned about the bigness we're getting and what we're doing to the small man. I hope somebody would remember that this is a growing problem which hasn't yet been addressed in this country.

*The Moderator asks Jake Pickle: Does Congress launch laws that are so ambiguous that Congress loses control of the administrative agencies set up to interpret and administer the laws?*

## Jake Pickle
*Congressman*

Congress responds to the requests of the people—for instance, to do something about the environment. That's what the Congress is trying to do. Congress isn't trying to write final, irrevocable laws. We didn't do that in the automobile emission standards. But we did do something, and it had to be done. If anybody has gone to somewhere like Tokyo and seen how that city is absolutely choked to death, you'd know we've got to do something about emissions. The government simply responds.

Sometimes we don't know what is best; neither does the automobile industry. Your own big companies were split right down the middle on the right approach to take concerning emission standards.

## Frank Ikard
*American Petroleum Institute*

The point made earlier concerning the independent agencies was that they were *not*, in fact, created, as their name implies, to have delegated legislative authority. They were created as independent agencies. Under their charter they were supposed to report to the Congress of the United States annually, in long, voluminous reports that nobody would read. They were to report about how they were handling their charge.

Now these agencies are in effect a fourth branch of government. I doubt that you have overview committees. The suggestion was made that an annual report should be required that would indicate publicly what direction the independent agency intended to pursue during the coming year.

I don't think Congress knows what the agencies are planning; this isn't meant as a criticism. Congress doesn't have the time to know. But this isn't anything business can get to. We both have indicated we've got problems with the bureaucracies.

## Jake Pickle
*Congressman*

Yes, there is a fourth form of government with respect to some of the agencies. This problem could be controlled by working through the Cabinet. The Cabinet approach could do it. The Director of the Department of the Interior could say, "This has got to be done." But you get over in the independent agencies, and there's not any boss, so that direction isn't easily taken.

## Charls Walker
*Charls E. Walker Associates, Inc.*

If you had ever been in the Cabinet, as I was as Assistant to the Secretary of the Treasury, and tried to control something like the Internal Revenue Service, you'd know you had yourself one . . . hard job!

Returning to the attitudes around the country, including that of this middle class I make so much of, we simply have to do a more effective job of increasing or raising the level of economic understanding and reducing the level of economic illiteracy.

We've done a brilliant job in this country with the three Rs (perhaps with the exception of writing at this stage of the game). We have done a tremendous job in education except in one glaring area: economics. There seems to be little understanding of what makes a market economy, especially a mixed economy, tick.

Let me tell you an anecdote. When I was working as Assistant to the Secretary of the Treasury back in 1959, interest rates had gone up, up, up. They had gone above two and a half percent, and above three percent on long-term government bonds.

They actually reached four and a half percent there in 1959; everybody was very uptight about that. It was going to kill everybody all over the country. We could not sell a government bond with an interest rate on it of more than four and a quarter percent—an old hangover from World War I that didn't make any sense at all.

President Eisenhower—Frank Ikard was on the Ways and Means Committee then, and I think he remembers this episode vividly—set up legislation to eliminate this ceiling so that we could finance a government debt.

One day Secretary Anderson and I were up on the Hill visiting a member from our part of the country, from an agricultural district. And Secretary Anderson took some time, about thirty or forty minutes, to explain why this interest rate ceiling should be removed. And he did it eloquently.

He said, "Joe, you know that we've got to borrow money. We've got to pay for the spending that you guys in Congress approve. If we can't borrow out at twenty or thirty years, we've got to borrow down at one or two years where we could pay the higher rates. That's inflationary; that's more like money, and it gets into the banks, and so on."

And he finished his peroration, and said, "What do you think, Joe?" And Joe said, "I agree with you one hundred percent."

Anderson asked, "Are you going to vote with me?"

Joe said, "Nope."

Secretary Anderson said, "Why not?"

Joe replied, "Bob, I'll level with you. I'll be running next autumn, and I'll be out in the district, and I'll drive down the road and see a farmer at the side of the road and pull over, and you know what the first thing he's going to ask me? 'Did you vote with Dwight Eisenhower for high interest rates or Wright Patman for low interest rates?' And I don't have forty-five minutes to explain to him why I voted with you."

How do we approach the problem of economic ignorance? Well, it's being approached already. You approach it in the secondary schools through such excellent programs as that of the Joint Committee on Economic Education, which I've been associated with for years. General Motors is one of the big supporters of this organization, as are others here in the room from the business community.

When the Joint Committee started in 1948 to see if a better job of teaching economics could be done in the high schools, the first thing they found was there weren't any teachers who could teach economics in the high schools. The program was devoted to teaching the teachers about economics. That has been very effective.

Colleges and universities are getting into teaching economics more and more, outside of departments of economics so engineers and general arts majors and others can be taught about economics. Some colleges, like my alma mater, have made mistakes. They created a Chair of Free Enterprise, which drove labor up the wall. Call it a "Chair of American Business" or a "Chair of Private Enterprise" or a "Chair on the Market Economy," or something.

These efforts to teach economics are spreading rapidly throughout the country, and doing an increasingly effective job. For that great "unwashed middle class," basic education has got to be done through the media. Here I throw a very strong criticism, not at Leonard Silk and *The New York Times,* not at *The Wall Street Journal,* not at most of the major newspapers around the country, where the quality of economic reporting and analysis is great, but at radio and particularly television, where it is absolutely lousy.

I firmly believe that television is responsible for convincing the American public in 1973 or 1974 that the oil crisis was manufactured by the major oil companies, and not a result of the Arab oil embargo. So, if you want to do something worthwhile, you will use every effort in the participatory democracy to raise the level of economic understanding and economic reporting (particularly by that part of the media most people get their news and information from).

> *The first question from the audience in this last discussion again launches the panelists into an examination of the nature of a possible business-government partnership. The European experience (rooted in feudalism, when business, government, and religion were closely entwined) differs considerably from American economic and political philosophy and reality. Does European business-*

223

*government solidarity provide European-based business an enviable competitive edge in the world market? How far can we in America emulate the European mode of business-government collaboration? These are some of the questions examined in the concluding discussion.*

## From the Audience:

Mr. Smith, I quote from your speech today: "We compete not only for customers in the marketplace but for influence in the world. To compete aggressively for either, we must have a closer alliance between business and government. It is, remember, an alliance that all industrial democracies in the world already enjoy."

What kind of industrial democracy enjoys this? We don't have free enterprise in Europe. I come from a representative Scandinavian country. We have a so-called mixed economy, where the cooperation between government and business has resulted in limiting and regulating the economy to the extreme. Neither the government nor business is making profits; in essence, we are soon going bankrupt, in spite of the oil.

Instead of using us as an example of how to do it, I would think you should see us as an example of how *not* to do it—to have partnership. Can you please explain a little bit more about what you mean by "enjoyment."

## Roger Smith
*General Motors Corporation*

Any businessman in the United States who participates in world trade would agree with what I said. We quite often, as a multinational company, find ourselves bidding in overseas markets. Just recently we bid on a locomotive for an African country. We had to finance the locomotives ourselves. The German bid, I think, came in with financing at four percent, as opposed to something around nine and a half percent needed to finance our bid. The Japanese bid was financed at three percent.

I'll tell you where they're getting that money. They're getting it from their governments. You'll find in most countries around the world—I'll take the European countries right down the line, Germany, France, and so on—are providing a unified front in world commerce. They have their businesses, their banks, and their industry right tight together to bid for world trade.

If you look and see what some of these countries are doing, you'll agree that the one free world market left in the world is the United States. I think there are a lot of countries that take advantage of that.

Some of these countries say, "Well, we've got an oversupply of steel (or something), we should probably lay off some of our steel workers." But instead, the government will go into the steel company and say, "You lower the price of steel, sell it to the United States, and we will subsidize you." In effect, what these countries are doing is exporting unemployment to the United States.

Certainly we have trade agreements. If Ambassador Strauss were here he could speak much more eloquently than I can on trade. But I say this to you: Our trading partners are very clever in nontariff trade barriers. The second largest car market in the world today is Japan. If my figures are right, fewer than 50,000 United States cars were sold into Japan last year.

How does that work? Well, the Japanese would tell you that they don't have any trade barriers; that they welcome our products. But I submit to you that when you go in there and find out it takes eighteen months to get a car certified for sale in Japan, you run into the so-called nontariff barriers they have.

There is no way that we are going to beat that system unless we as a country get our act together to get business, labor, the government, and our financing institutions into an equally tight partnership so we can compete in the markets.

Regarding the Scandinavian markets: maybe some of the way they've handled it up there, even though a cooperative effort, has been a failure because they've been following the wrong policies. But I submit to you again, they are allied much more closely than we are; they just haven't embarked on a good course.

## Jake Pickle
*Congressman*

Two or three years ago this matter came up before our committee: How can we compensate American employees overseas so they can get some kind of tax deduction for going over to work, so they will stay there?

When I proposed legislation two years ago everyone thought it was on behalf of a Texas company, and we didn't even get enough votes to get mad about it. Now, in the space of two years, the public has begun to understand. Some of Charls Walker's friends have gone around individually to see many of the Congressmen who said it was nothing but a ripoff for these big companies and their employees.

Now some realize that the only way we can be competitive in the world market is for our government to help make us competitive. One vehicle is to help make it possible for American companies to operate overseas. Congress passed a bill just last year giving some tax relief for Americans working in foreign countries.

But I would not want to leave you the impression we want to put ourselves on a level of "enjoying the same comforts of other nations." I don't want to enjoy those same comforts. The United States is the most completely free enterprise nation in the world. We don't have any businesses in the country that the government owns (although we're getting mighty close in the case of the railroad). That's not true in any other country in Europe, Asia, or anywhere else.

## From the Audience:

We've been talking about existing business-government conflicts. Jake Pickle pointed out that business is not complaining about government as much as the bureaucracy and the conflicts that arise there. If we're going to work toward a government and a business partnership, and have participatory democracy, we do need voter stimulation. We cannot have a business-government partnership until the voters participate.

How do you stimulate that participation? We spend millions of dollars, probably billions of dollars, on campaigns in order to get people to come out and vote. It's not working.

I think the true partnership will have to be not only government and business and labor, and as you all indicated, the voters, too. I would like to know at what point it will become necessary to each of you, as representatives of government and business, to demonstrate that you all can make valid decisions, or use rational processes, only if you're informed. By what sort of process can you demonstrate to us, the voters, that our participation is valid.

**Frank Ikard**
*American Petroleum Institute*

Remember the Pennsylvania election of last November, where one House seat was decided by one vote? That event clearly indicates every vote counts. Maybe that's an overly simple answer. In all kinds of situations voter participation shows up as the essence of the decisionmaking process in a democracy.

**John Gardner**
*Educator and Statesman*

There are innumerable examples of the effectiveness of voter participation. I do *not* think you can throw the weight on our representative institutions by saying they've got to come up with perfect answers. They've got to be responsive; they've got to face up to what the voters are concerned about. The capacity of the voter to get the message across has been proven and reproven. The most startling recent example, of course, is Proposition 13. But from where I sit, and I watch Congress pretty closely, Congress is the accessible branch. If you want to participate, you can reach them faster than you can reach anybody else.

## Jake Pickle
*Congressman*

People may not participate in some elections, and sometimes their interest is a little bit lower than others. But basically, all you've got to do is get people to get mad; then they'll turn out. If you let the wrong political party come in office, then the good people will come in and get it straightened out.

I'm not disillusioned that you have to prove participation over and over again. If the public gets interested and involved, they'll turn out. We can't force it; but the process is generally working all right.

## From the Audience:

Concerning the importance of participation in the political parties, I think the political parties—the Democratic and Republican and others—set the policy and the tone for the nominations of the candidates.

I know I come from a precinct that votes about five hundred to a thousand votes each election. When we have a precinct convention after that, it is usually attended by less than eleven people. I know we get eleven members to go to the county convention. Now, we sometimes don't have enough people there to nominate the people to go to the county convention! This is where you've got to start. If you really want to participate in politics, go to your precinct convention, right at the ground level. I presume that most of you know what a precinct convention is.

## From the Audience:

Congressman Pickle, do you have any suggestions for an innovative incentive to eliminate paper, such as an extra week's vacation for each ton saved?

## Jake Pickle
*Congressman*

Well, yes. We ought to pass fewer regulatory laws; we're the ones that start them, we launch them. Second, we ought to have a law that says you can't have but one page of a regulation. I think shortening the forms would be a big help. But most of all, I hope that when they ask for information they go to the substantive issues, and not try to answer a hundred things when five would take care of the basic thrust of the legislation passed. If we put that over to the bureaucracy, that would help as much as anything.

**From the Audience:**

Isn't it true that most of the agencies generate most of their own information? That there's really not much sharing of information going on between these agencies, and so the businessman ends up sending the same information to ten different agencies? Couldn't there be one agency to collect the information from which the agencies could draw?

**Jake Pickle**
*Congressman*

Yes. You've got a good point. There's a great deal of duplication. Each agency has its own little turf. It's hard to overcome. That's something we are trying to work on. It's a big problem to cut back.

**From the Audience:**

In reference to the public and the government not being able to communicate effectively, is someone in government studying the potential of commercial television in prime time in a question-and-response-type situation?

**Jake Pickle**
*Congressman*

Well, I would say yes—in the first place, whatever kind of study there is, the government has got it going somewhere.

**From the Audience:**

Is it technically possible to transmit a public forum to the average American citizen today, and receive back from each household a "yes" or "no" response?

## Jake Pickle
*Congressman*

Yes, it's possible. I don't know if I can put my finger on exactly how we are studying it. Public television is one good vehicle for that. A great deal is going on: extensive discussions of matters before the government and how they're handled, and who's right and who's wrong.

Let me tell you one of the most difficult things we have in the Congress—we don't know what the people are really thinking. You get elected, but keeping in touch is very difficult. I could go to a precinct and say we're going to have a town hall meeting. I have about six to eight of these in different parts of the city all through the year. I'll put out notices, I'll make phone calls. If we get fifty people to come, we're lucky. They don't want to cut into whatever television program is on that night.

Keeping in touch with them is very difficult. I've got a questionnaire that I'm sending out. It's in the mail now. I'll announce: you'll all be getting it within the next week. I limit it to thirty-six questions. I want people to respond. I try to say, "Answer me yes or no." People are hungry, though, to express themselves. They write, not just yes or no, they write "yes" and "no" and "but." They write me two or three pages on it. That's wonderful, but sorting through twenty thousand questionnaires is very difficult, even if interesting.

## Frank Ikard
*American Petroleum Institute*

Beginning this week, they're televising the proceedings of the House of Representatives. Cable television, as I understand it, has a contract to deliver that to every community that has cable television. They will have periods during the day—this is not commercial—where you can view the excitement of the house floor.

## Charls Walker
*Charls E. Walker Associates, Inc.*

I hope nothing comes out of it; it is not the role of the

federal government to put on a forum and then push a button and see how the people out there respond to it. I've got grave doubts of just how balanced that forum is going to be. It would be, I guess, if the Republicans took over again.

I've been associated off and on over the past seven or eight years with a show known as "The Advocates" out of WGBH in Boston. They'll take an hour and air both sides of an issue very effectively. The audience for that show tends to be stacked toward what I would call the liberal side. But if you can have a full ventilation of an issue, people will listen. For example, John Swearingen and I were on the show in 1975. A Senator of the United States had produced a bill in the Congress to establish a federal oil and gas corporation, which was a stacked deck if there ever was a stacked deck. As a result of the debate on that show, despite the nature of the audience I knew was out there, the respondents—some twenty thousand who watched and sent in postcards—said two to one that they were against what John Swearingen and I referred to as "FOGCO," the Federal Oil and Gas Corporation.

These sorts of things are happening, but I want them to happen out there in the private sector. I don't mean necessarily the for-profit private sector; there's a role public television can serve, and should serve, a lot better.

**John Gardner**
*Educator and Statesman*

Everybody is worried about the word "partnership." A really good partnership could be a terrible bear hug—you might regret that you'd gotten into it. The question raised by the young lady from the Scandinavian country is relevant here. All kinds of modes of intervention and modes of relationship between the federal government and the private sector have occurred over and over again since colonial days. Yet we haven't been very analytical about which ones are workable and which ones aren't.

The business world goes right back into very binding relationships with government. So does the academic world, nonprofit world, the professions, and so on. No one has any analytical sense of what modes of relationship are imprisoning and destroying the viability of the private sector, or of what relationships enable it to do the job that it can do best.

We ought to undertake to be more analytical about the various kinds of relations. Not just say we should have a closer, or less close, relationship, but to say let's look at the way they relate. The Reconstruction Finance Corporation idea, for example, done correctly, could result in an enabling and enhancing kind of relationship.

### Frank Ikard
*American Petroleum Institute*

Yes, to reiterate, before we can attack or reach any of these problems we somehow have to develop a new spirit of confidence, of participation. I think too many of us—and I'm not usually a pessimist—feel that we've kind of lost control.

We feel somewhat overwhelmed by the present and unable to do anything about the future. We've got to get this behind us. I suspect that this is the residue of Vietnam and Watergate, and of all those traumatic things that we've just lived through. If we can develop our communications and our confidence in each other, business's confidence in government, and government's confidence, then we can talk in a more rational way.

### Jake Pickle
*Congressman*

One of our most overriding needs is to increase the level of risk taking. Encouraging risk taking might take the form of reducing a tax on capital gains from investments in new businesses, maybe allowing investors in new businesses to deduct those businesses' losses from personal income, as we do now for partnerships. We might even have a reciprocal excess-profit tax.

I am disturbed that businesses seem to get bigger and bigger. I like to read about the five hundred major corporations in the United States, because they must do well. They are our bread and butter. But the bread and butter of this country is also the tens upon thousands of small businesses gradually being strangled by paperwork or bought up by big business. We're going to be faced someday with horizontal and vertical divestiture if we're going to keep the small business.

That may sound like a bit of hypocrisy or wild dreaming, but we can't let the big companies keep buying the little ones up and taking a write-off. Because that does affect productivity. We're going to see something done about that, because the vast business enterprise of the United States is the small people, tens of thousands of them all across the country. We're driving them out of business because they can't fill out the forms, and they look for a way to escape. Such a trend can destroy the very foundation of American free enterprise if we don't do something about it.

**Charls Walker**
*Charls E. Walker Associates, Inc.*

Let's back up a minute to what John Gardner and the young lady from Scandinavia said about partnership.

There is no question that a government-business partnership, in a country where the "Establishment" (most often it's a parliamentary democracy) consists mainly of the business community, at least in day-to-day affairs, can be tremendously effective in a pure economic sense. The two strongest cases of that are West Germany and Japan. We made a decision in this country that we don't want to go that way to get economic progress at the cost that sort of partnership would entail. We made that decision a long time ago.

Our solution to this will be a typically American type of solution. You will have a blending and an amalgamation of the different notions of partnership which are emerging from this symposium.

**Roger Smith**
*General Motors Corporation*


If you think that the disappearance of small companies is due to big businesses buying up, you really ought to take another hard look. General Motors hasn't bought a business in twenty-five years, and we've grown fairly well in spite of that. But we have 45,000 small companies that supply us, and they're vital to our strength.

What's happened to the small companies are two things. You've got your finger on one of them. They can no longer put up with filling in the four hundred forms required by government. More importantly, they've been forced out of business by international competition. There's not another company in the United States today other than General Motors that assembles radios. The radios in the United States are being assembled outside our country. Why? Because they are not competitive in the world market. Why aren't they competitive? To a great extent because of the pressure and cost of government regulation put on them here that the competitor in the Far East does not have.

If we want to keep small business viable in this country, we ought to take a close look at our international policies and our cost of government regulation. Last year government regulation cost General Motors—I'm not talking about hardware or anything—1.2 billion dollars. There are not many companies that can afford that. We can't afford it ourselves.

I'm not discouraged; there can be a great partnership. The great promise of America is yet to come. And there is plenty of energy if we pursue a reasonable, rational energy policy. Only our government can direct that for us. There is so much at stake in our future that depends on the government that we have to have a good alliance, a word I prefer to "partnership." If you go back to the roots of what made our country great in the old days, you'll find it was freedom. We've got to get back to that, if we are to achieve the promise we have ahead of us.

## From the Audience:

The conference as a whole has been excellent, but something is missing. I'm going to direct my remarks to Mr. Ikard.

No one in the symposium took the point of view that something more might exist between the government and business—perhaps a Socialist point of view: going all the way to national planning. I'm not espousing those views; I'm only saying that such a perspective might have added a different dimension to this very provocative discussion. Mr. Ikard talked about how people, having once participated, back away because they find they are not listened to. What about those who aren't participating yet?

## Frank Ikard
*American Petroleum Institute*

I hope I said nothing to indicate that I favored central planning. I did try to indicate the importance, in the energy field and other areas, of establishing some kind of national direction and national goals; this is essential.

It would have been interesting to have someone espouse the central planning viewpoint, but I'm not your man.

## From the Audience:

Congressman Pickle, thank you very much for your remarks. Have you conceived, or is government promoting, a system by which recognition could be given to people who come up with innovative ideas to cut the inflationary tendencies of the private sector?

## Jake Pickle
*Congressman*

I don't know what the government is doing specifically on that. The President has proposed a real wage insurance. He's going to give you credit if you keep your inflation rate down to a certain level. But that's not flying very fast right now. And I don't know if the government is actually doing anything else along these lines, or whether it should or not.

*As questions from the audience become more scattered, the time allotted for the last session comes to an end. The Moderator provides a helpful capstone.*

# Moderator's Capstone

**Walt W. Rostow**
*Professor of Economics
and History,*
The University of Texas
at Austin

*The Moderator for the final panel discussion, Dr. Walt W. Rostow, has been a professor of economics and history at The University of Texas at Austin since 1969. A former adviser to Presidents John F. Kennedy and Lyndon B. Johnson, Dr. Rostow's career spans education, scholarship, and government service. A prolific author, his most recent books are* The World Economy: History and Prospect *(1978) and* Getting from Here to There *(1978).*

*Professor Rostow sums up the elements involved in the notion of partnership which has emerged from the symposium as a whole.*

What are the elements in the notion of a new partnership? We seem to have identified three. First is the "Alexander Hamilton notion," or the Federalist notion. Namely, one part of the partnership would consist of the government creating an environment through political leadership and attitudes, fiscal monetary policy, possibly tax incentives, which would make it possible for the private sector to perform the role it is supposed to perform in our society. The powerful moves of our government to establish

237

a uniform currency and unify the country economically created an environment for private enterprise by giving confidence to investors.

The second element brought up in relation to the notion of partnership developed here at this symposium might be linked with Benjamin Cardoza, since it concerns excessive bureaucratic regulations. Mr. Cardoza, in his concurring opinion on the Schechter case, which declared the National Recovery Act unconstitutional, described that original piece of legislation and its aftermath as "delegation run wild." Excessive bureaucratic regulations have preoccupied us throughout this conference. Public servants have once again, it seems, been delegated powers over which there are no checks. Pulling back, or reconciling conflicting administrative rulings based on different laws, is a possibility mentioned more than once during our discussions here.

The third element involved in the notion of partnership emerging from the symposium might be named after Jesse Jones: The identification of areas in which positive collaboration is required between the public and the private sectors. A big part of our difficulty in solving national problems results from the *absence* of a framework in which private enterprise can do its job without violating equity or other canons of our society. Those of us involved in this symposium seem to agree there's a place for public-private collaboration in solving the overriding priority problems of this society—energy, inflation, salvation of the dollar, trade, productivity—those great household tasks of the nation.

If there has been a fourth notion of partnership running through these sessions, from the eloquence of Felix Rohatyn at the beginning to the appeal of Roger Smith at the end, it is the need for a new spirit of cooperation. The nature of faction in a democratic society has long been debated, from the Federalist Papers and the Constitutional Convention of 1787, to Washington's Farewell Address—a plea against factionalism and its dangers—to the examination of special interests and pluralism made here today. To achieve any kind of partnership among the various sectors of society, we need a communal purpose.

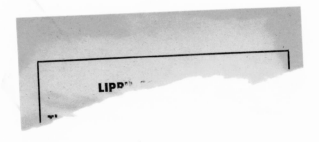

LIPP